BABY'S FIRST YEAR MILESTONES

Promote & Celebrate
Your Baby's Development with
MONTHLY GAMES & ACTIVITIES

Aubrey Hargis

Foreword by David L. Hill, MD, FAAP
Illustrations by Turine Tran

ROCKRIDGE
PRESS

Designer: Christopher T. Fong
Editor: Katie Moore
Production Editor: Erum Khan
Illustrations © Turine Tran, 2018
Cover photography © Sirtravelalot/Shutterstock

ISBN: Print 978-1-64152-051-5 | eBook 978-1-64152-052-2

TO MY MOTHER,
whose constant admiration of
babies was evidently contagious.

CONTENTS

FOREWORD

As a pediatrician, every day I answer a lot of different questions from parents. Many of them involve poop. Many others involve rashes. Sometimes they involve both. But underlying every question I answer is one overarching concern: "Is my baby okay?" After that, "Is my baby going to stay okay?" and then, "How can I help?"

Concerns about poop and rashes, however, pale when compared to anxiety over development, especially in the first year of life. Somewhere there is an infant who crawled at six months, walked at nine months, and spoke in full sentences in time to sing along with "Happy Birthday to You." And for some reason, everyone knows that baby. If you're that baby's parent, by the way, please stop telling people about him.

Chances are, though, your baby is developing normally and will get better every day. If you don't believe me, just keep reading this book. Aubrey Hargis has done an amazing job of condensing the conversations that I have with parents all day long into a simple, clear, fun-to-read guide that will have you playing and singing with your baby all year long.

An enormous and highly profitable industry has sprung up around infant development. To browse a baby catalog you'd think that unless you spend a small college fund on specially designed toys, both digital and analog, there's no point in even starting a college fund. While I'll be the first to agree that many of these toys are so adorable that I want to play with them myself (seriously, don't you ever look at a cool teething ring and sort of wish you could teethe again, just for a day?), your baby doesn't need any of these things in order to develop: She needs only you.

On the flip side, there are many servers' worth of information on social media devoted to making your own baby toys with nothing more than several bolts of colorful felt, some empty cans of steel-cut organic oats, a few hand-turned dowels made from reclaimed antique oak, and a dozen discarded champagne corks, along with access to a high-speed jigsaw and a professional-grade glue gun. Feel free to go there if you want, but this is not that book, either. There are a few scarves and tissue boxes scattered here and there, but you can do without them, too. Mainly you just need yourself and a baby.

What I love most about this book is that it's fun. Caring for an infant is hard work (have I mentioned the poop and the rashes?), but it's also thoroughly delightful. Aubrey has gone out of her way on every page to amplify that delight. So read, play, sing, enjoy.

—David L. Hill, MD, FAAP

WELCOME TO YEAR ONE!

All great stories have a beginning. The story of your baby's life is happening right now. Within the span of 12 months, your newborn will transform from a tiny creature intensely dependent upon you for survival into an active, expressive child with clear interests and preferences. Just as soon as you notice a new behavior or skill, another has already started to develop.

It's a story worth celebrating every step of the way. By your baby's first birthday, she may be pointing out topics for conversation, waving bye-bye, and speaking a few first words. Her fingers will be adept enough to pick up a small piece of food, and she may even have taken her first steps.

So how do all of these changes actually happen? It is through play that children grow and learn. All babies are born with the strong instinct to play in specific ways that allow them to develop motor, sensory, language, and social-emotional skills. Playing with your baby is the best thing you can do to help her learn, and it's also a lot of fun!

You will be able to tell what your baby is learning by being aware of her developmental milestones. They do occur at a fairly rapid pace, although always on a baby's own schedule, as well as in a recognizable progression. The leaps and bounds that babies will make in a year are the result of an absolutely incredible amount of brain growth. In fact, throughout this first year, a baby's brain typically forms more than a million new neural connections every second, and it is also the most flexible and adaptive it will ever be.

Many parents worry about how to properly nurture their baby's potential to the fullest. Rest assured, your baby will be learning an unimaginable amount just by being with you. As you hold her, feed her, talk to her, and play games together, you will be helping her learn all about the world and learning how to communicate with each other. Every time you observe her movements, respond to her vocalizations, and seek to understand her needs, you are learning more about who she is as a person and helping promote her development.

Whether you are spending time with your baby throughout the day, in the morning as you are getting ready to go to work, while grocery shopping, on weekends, or in the car while traveling, your baby is learning and growing so much just by interacting with you. When you want to try a new way to play, this book can be your go-to source. The wide variety of simple activities and games are designed to be as entertaining as they are educational—complementing each month's milestones, highlights, and challenges. Consider trying a few new ones each month, and be prepared to repeat the ones that your baby loves the most. In fact, expect her to insist on that. Repetition makes her feel secure while she naturally practices important skills. As you experiment with different routines, activities, and techniques, you will find your own rhythm.

With love for your baby, trust in the natural unfolding of human development, and, resources in hand, you will learn to navigate the ups and downs of this first year. There is no one "right" way to be a parent. You will always be the real expert on your own unique, precious baby.

How to Use This Book

This book covers your baby's first year month by month. Here's what you'll find in each chapter.

Introduction

Each chapter opens with:

- An overview of what to expect that month
- Typical behavioral challenges
- Highlights to look forward to

Developmental Milestones and Games and Activities

Next comes the heart of this book: typical developmental milestones for each month paired with complementary games for you and your baby to play together. To help you more deeply understand your baby's rapid changes, the milestones and activities are divided into four categories:

- Motor skills
- Sensory development
- Language and mental development
- Social-emotional skills

Each category starts with an overview and describes that month's major milestones. Then the fun really begins! The activities that follow the milestones have a twofold purpose:

- To support your baby's development through age-appropriate play
- To inspire you and your baby to play together in different ways

Babies develop skills through play and interacting with loved ones—most especially you. These activities are designed to be as fun for the two of you as they are educational. Pick and choose the ones that appeal to you, and feel free to customize them and make them your own. Your baby's smiles, laughter, and obvious desire to do an activity again will tell you which are the keepers. If she turns away, isn't interested, or even becomes unhappy, stop the activity and consider it again the next month, or just move on to find her favorites. It's all about you having fun together, not the number of activities you do. If you find just a few gems—or even just one—you've succeeded. This book is intended to bring pleasure, not pressure, into your life.

Sidebars

Extra insights, solutions for common concerns, and certain aspects of your daily life with your baby are covered in sidebars.

Notes

At the end of each chapter, you'll find prompts for notes and space to jot down favorite moments and memories from the month.

Extras at the End of the Book

After the "Month 12" chapter are three sections designed for your personal reference.

- A comprehensive list of the major milestones with a place to check off each one and record the date. Because every baby follows an individual path of development, this record-keeping section lists milestones in a general sequence rather than by month.
- A list of milestones that your baby's doctor will cover at well-baby checkups.
- A notes section where you can write down some of your favorite memories of your baby's first year.

IMPORTANT NOTE: YOUR BABY'S OWN TIMELINE

This book describes developmental milestones in the sequence in which they typically occur. No one can tell you exactly when your baby will be able to master a specific skill. This is because babies are unique creatures with genetic predispositions, strong personalities, and different strengths. No baby follows an exactly predictable timeline.

When it comes to growth in the first year, normal ranges of development span several months for the mastery of each milestone. Your baby may be early for some milestones and later for others, and this is perfectly normal. In this book, most will be listed on the early side of the normal range, so keep this in mind if your child hasn't quite reached one yet. Patience will be your friend this year.

If your late bloomer still hasn't mastered a skill and the later side of the typical range has passed, you may want to bring this up at your baby's next checkup. Doctors are used to listening to parental concerns and will be able to assess your child's development and offer guidance. It's always a good idea to ask for a professional opinion if you are wondering whether your baby is on track, but given the wide range of normal behavior, the chances are very good that your baby just needs a bit more time to grow.

MONTH

1

Your Baby This Month

There is no one better than you to introduce your newborn to the world. But with so much time devoted to basic needs—feeding, diapering, soothing, and getting your baby to sleep—it may seem like there's not a lot you can do with your newborn. Rest assured, every time you interact with your baby—talk, sing, hold, touch, move around—you are doing something very important. Your newborn already has many capabilities that help her adjust to the outside world, such as the abilities to suck and swallow and to focus on your face as you cradle her.

A newborn's ears have been able to hear voices and other sounds since about 12 weeks before birth. She is actively listening to you when you speak and sing to her. During these first weeks together, you and your baby are getting to know and understand each other, and it may seem like your little one is constantly changing—because she is! She's taking it all in and benefiting from every minute with you.

Challenges This Month

- **Crying:** Babies cry to let us know that they need us in some way. Your baby might be hungry, need a diaper change, want to be held, be overstimulated, or just want to cry for some mysterious reason that you'll never figure out. Some babies are fussier than others, and in general, crying itself is not harmful. The important thing to remember is that when you respond to your baby's cries, you are teaching a valuable lesson: I care.
- **Feeding:** How much and how often? There's only one person who truly knows, and that's your baby. Watch for hunger cues, including making smacking sounds, sucking on hands, and fussing. When you offer breast milk or formula, your baby can choose to accept or refuse. You'll also notice your baby's head turning away when finished. On average, babies this age need to eat every two to three hours.
- **Sleeping:** Newborns sleep about 16 hours a day, spaced throughout the day and night. In these early weeks, keep periods of wakefulness brief—30 to 90 minutes. Pay attention to learn your baby's subtle cues that she's tired—reduced activity, staring off, droopy eyelids—and try to get her to a dark, quiet environment and ready for sleep before she becomes overtired. Ironically, being overtired makes it harder for a baby to get to sleep.

Highlights This Month

- **Getting to know each other:** Hold your baby and talk to her. She's learning that she has a parent who cares.
- **Feeding:** You may be breastfeeding. While nursing is natural, that doesn't mean that it's easy, and getting a good latch can be tricky. If you're breastfeeding and have any trouble, ask your baby's doctor or a lactation consultant for help right away.
- **First bath:** It takes a couple of weeks for the umbilical cord stump to fall off, but when it does, it's time for a nice warm bath.
- **Finding what works:** Practice a variety of techniques—rocking, bouncing, swaying, or mastering the colic hold—for soothing crying. Do what works for your newborn.

Motor Skills

Your newborn may look relatively helpless at birth, but in fact your baby already has superpowers. The drive to move one's arms and legs in sync in preparation for walking is already part of your baby's secret mission. Expect movements to be quite jerky and unrefined, though they will soon smooth out. The sucking instinct is strong, and those cheek muscles will bulk up, too.

Self-confidence begins right from the start as you support your baby's urge to move and appreciate the hard work it takes to accomplish each feat. Playtime is simple and more about quiet bonding times than romping around.

Milestones

- **Has strong reflexes:** Your baby can already do so much! You'll notice your baby rooting by turning a cheek when touched, sucking strongly, grasping your finger, startling at loud noises, extending an arm or leg when turning the head to the side, and picking up her feet when held upright over a smooth surface. These instinctual survival reflexes are hardwired into your baby's brain.
- **Turns head side to side while lying on stomach:** Your baby's neck muscles are not as strong as they will be someday, but they are already working hard to turn his neck from side to side. This takes a lot of practice.
- **Lifts head for a second while lying on stomach:** Before your baby can learn to sit up or crawl, the neck muscles must be able to support that heavy head. You may notice your baby straining to lift up just a tiny bit. The action may seem small, but it takes enormous effort.
- **Makes jerky, quivering arm thrusts:** Your baby's arm movements are not smooth and refined. Instead, expect some flailing about. This is normal.
- **Keeps hands in tight fists:** Because of the grasping reflex, stroking your baby's hand triggers a tight fist. Those little fingers will soon unfold in order to explore, but just like a good swaddle, staying tucked in is the most comfortable position for now.
- **Flops head backward if unsupported:** The neck muscles are working hard to get stronger, but you need to consistently provide extra support for your baby's head.
- **Brings hands within range of eyes and mouth:** Inside the womb, your baby spent most of the time curled up tight with both hands near his face. Look for fist-sucking behavior, which is an indicator that your baby is hungry.

Games and Activities

You Got Me!

Feel firsthand your baby's grasping reflex, which allows him to hug your finger.

1. Touch your baby's palm gently with one of your own fingers. His fingers will close around your finger.
2. Stay in this position for as long as it feels good to both of you.
3. When he releases the hold, gently extract your finger.

Tummy Cuddles

Tummy time doesn't have to be on the floor. You can do it right where baby is nestled in comfort—with you.

1. Say to your baby, "Let's have a tummy cuddle."
2. In a temperate climate, remove your baby's clothing down to the diaper, talking about your actions as you go.
3. Find a comfortable position in a reclining chair or slightly propped up with pillows on a sofa.

Continues on page 6.

TUMMY TIME

Tummy time allows your baby to stretch and explore the way muscles move in different positions, but it might not always be comfortable. He has a natural drive to lift up his head, but it's hard work.

Newborns are not able to change positions on their own yet, so it is up to you to help. The time to practice is while he is in an alert, awake state of consciousness. And it doesn't need to last very long. Observe to identify when that work is going well and when it is just plain frustrating. When he gets tired or overstimulated, move on to something else.

Here are a few things you can do to assist in the process:

Try Tummy Cuddles (see page 4) first. Having your warm body underneath as she tries to lift her head is a gentle, comfortable way for most babies to begin tummy time.

Allow your baby lots of freedom of movement. Swaddling can calm a fussing baby, and being strapped into a car seat is required when in a moving vehicle, but the majority of days and nights your baby should be in an uninhibited environment—for example, in your arms, on the floor, or in a stretchy baby carrier.

Get on the floor with your baby sometimes. It is a rare baby who likes to be planted on the floor facedown and then left alone. Nose to nose or side by side, have a little gazing time, sing, tell a story, or just talk about your day.

Show your baby something to look at, such as a toy. Having something interesting to look at stimulates her mentally.

Place your baby horizontally on your lap. This is also a great position for burping a newborn because it provides a little pressure on the belly. Put on some soft music and gently pat your baby's back to the beat while your baby practices lifting and turning her head from side to side.

Continued from page 4.

4. Remove or open your shirt enough to expose your chest.
5. Place your calm and awake baby vertically on top of your chest so that your chin is just above her head. Your baby's knees may be bent with feet tucked in. This is fine.
6. Cover your baby up to the shoulders with a soft blanket.
7. Now relax and breathe deeply as she works those neck muscles to lift and stretch.

The skin-to-skin contact helps you and your baby bond as you warm up under the cozy blanket.

Supported Bounce

Gentle movements are soothing to newborns, so give this time-tested technique a try.

1. Lift your baby up slowly while fully supporting his neck.
2. Position his head on your shoulder with one hand and support his bottom with the other.
3. Standing with your feet shoulder width apart, bend your knees and let them slightly give to jiggle your body up and down.
4. Over the next several minutes, experiment to find a rhythm that your baby enjoys.
5. Vary the activity with sways, twists, and dips. Just make sure to keep one of your hands supporting his head, as babies can startle and flop backward unexpectedly.

Sensory Development

The human senses pave the way for all future learning. It is through your baby's eyes, ears, nose, mouth, and skin that the world becomes real. Every sight, sound, smell, taste, or touch forms connections in the brain. And senses are heightened in developmental stages for specific learning opportunities.

A baby's senses will not be exactly like those of an adult for quite some time, and this is a very good thing. Only the information and experiences that are essential for the current stage of development will be available for your child to learn from until the next stage begins. This allows your baby to focus and concentrate on unique, isolated sensations. For example, your baby is not able to focus on very faraway objects. This confines a baby's view to something that is much, much more important to get to know intimately: your face.

Offer a variety of experiences to stimulate your baby's senses, but don't go over-board. Newborns are easily overstimulated, and after a few minutes of engagement, your baby will let you know when it's time to stop.

Milestones

- **Focuses 8 to 12 inches away:** Your baby's vision is not yet developed well enough to focus on objects farther than about 8 to 12 inches away. Hold your baby in the cradle position and you'll notice that this exact distance allows your baby to clearly view the most important person in the world: you!
- **Tracks moving objects at close range (eyes might wander and occasionally cross):** Your baby's nearsighted eyes are cued in to large movements in the surrounding area. Bringing an object into close range and moving it slowly across your baby's field of vision likely attracts your baby's attention.
- **Prefers black-and-white or high-contrast patterns:** Your baby is most attracted to objects and pictures that feature dark patterns against a light background (or vice versa).
- **Sensitive to bright light:** Bright lights can be uncomfortable for a newborn's eyes, so provide an environment with dimmer light or plenty of shade. This doesn't mean that you need to live in darkness; giving your newborn a chance to experience the difference between daytime and nighttime light helps your baby know that aside from waking to feed, nighttime should primarily be for sleeping.
- **Cries, startles, or quiets with loud noises:** A newborn's ears are fairly well developed at birth, but now the sounds are crisp, clear, and quite sharp, as opposed to the muffled sounds experienced during the previous nine months. Your baby is likely to react with surprise at unexpected loud sounds. In contrast, you might notice your newborn's interest in hearing more nuanced, softer tones.
- **Has a highly tuned sense of smell:** Your baby is constantly sniffing for the sweet smell of milk, which naturally contains relatively high amounts of sugar. You might notice that your baby exhibits interest in sweet or fruity smells and may give a tiny nose wrinkle at bitter or acidic smells.
- **Has a well-developed sense of taste:** A newborn's taste buds are quite refined already. Not surprisingly, the preference is for sweet milk. Your baby can distinguish between warm and cool temperatures, too.
- **Prefers soft sensations:** Newborn skin is sensitive from head to toe, and your baby may settle more easily when directly touching your skin or a soft blanket. Coarse textures feel unpleasant.
- **Prefers gentle handling:** Move slowly and deliberately when you're holding your baby. Try gentle rocking, jiggling, or bouncing to calm him.

Games and Activities

Ting-a-Ling Sounds

While your newborn is in a quiet, alert state, introduce a high-pitched, softly ringing musical sound to stimulate your baby's ears. You need an instrument that chimes—a jingle bell, handbell, wind chime, piano key, or spoon and glass.

1. Tell your baby that you'd like her to hear a new sound.
2. Chime the sound once and wait a few seconds for your baby to process it. If she reacts positively, proceed. If not, take a break and try at another time.
3. If she seems to be listening, chime the sound three times in a row, waiting a few seconds again to let silence settle in.
4. Continue while she is enjoying it. When she turns away from the sound or seems agitated, put away your instrument and move on to something else.

Watch the Rainbow

A rainbow in space helps your baby work on visual tracking skills.

1. Hold a small object in your hand on one side of your baby's head.
2. Make eye contact with him and ask, "Would you like to watch this?"
3. Making sure to stay within your baby's visual focusing range (8 to 12 inches away), slowly move the object in an arc from one side to the other.
4. Note whether he is able to follow the path of the object.
5. Try slower and faster movements in order to find the optimal speed.
6. Don't worry if he is not adept at this game at first. This skill will become more and more developed every month.

Stargazing

Making goo-goo eyes gives your baby a chance to practice holding eye contact.

1. Hold your baby in a cradle position with the crook of your elbow nestling her head.
2. Now capture her gaze by saying out loud, "I love you."
3. Hold the gaze for as long as she is also continuing to make eye contact.
4. When she looks away, you can end the game or try to start it all over again with another "I love you."

It's Gotta Be Bold

Newborns are attracted to high-contrast or black-and-white patterns.

1. Find an object—a mobile, a board book, a piece of artwork, or even a dark object against a white background—with a high-contrast or black-and-white pattern.
2. Start by saying, "I'd like to show you something."
3. Position your baby—for example, in your lap or on the floor during tummy time—where he can see the pattern.
4. Allow him to gaze at the pattern as long as desired.

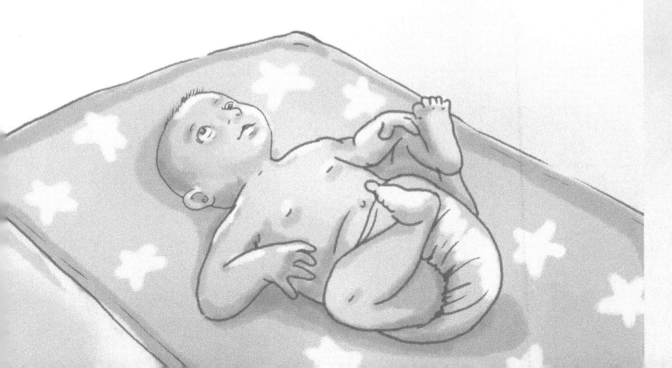

Language and Mental Development

A newborn's receptive language skills are already kicked into high gear. Babies are able to discriminate among all of the world's speech sounds, called phonemes. When you talk to your baby, she is identifying and categorizing the phonemes that make up the words and intonations in your language. Through exposure alone, the language you are speaking right now will become her native tongue.

You and your baby both have a job to do: figure out how to communicate with each other. Sometimes this will be an exceedingly easy task. Your natural instincts for nurturing will take over. Soothing your baby and understanding what is needed will feel almost effortless. During other times, it will be a frustrating endeavor, and you may feel helpless and inadequate. All of this is very normal. It will take time for the two of you to learn each other's cues and preferences.

Milestones

- **Cries to communicate needs:** Your baby communicates with you in many non-verbal ways, and if you tune in closely, you may be able to quickly put a finger on what he needs. A new diaper? Something to eat? A change in scenery? However, if your baby feels that you just aren't "getting it" or responding quickly enough, the sucking noises and soft fussing give way to a loud wail that you simply cannot ignore. It happens to every parent, no matter how attentive you are, so try to just go with the flow. Sometimes the reason a baby is crying remains a mystery, and that's okay.
- **Turns face away to indicate preferences:** Your little baby already has likes and dislikes. For example, if you are breastfeeding, he turns toward you to indicate hunger and away when finished eating. You may notice that the same is true with sweet and sour smells or bright lights and dark areas.
- **Calms when held, snuggled, or touched gently:** If your baby appears anxious or agitated, sometimes all that is needed is a gentle touch. When you respond to crying with warm, positive affection, you are letting your baby know that you are ready and willing to protect and assist when needed. This is how trust begins, and the bond between the two of you solidifies.

- **May be soothed by low, rhythmic tones:** Babies find low, rhythmic tones especially comforting during this first month. A favorite position for many newborns is right under your chin, where the vibrations of your vocal cords can be felt and your heart-beat is audible.
- **Can distinguish the speech sounds in human language:** Right from birth, your baby is attuned to the sounds that make up your voice and other voices she hears. Over the next several months, the sounds that are unused will become irrelevant, and your baby will begin babbling to you with the sounds of your language.

Games and Activities

A Lullaby for My Baby

There's a reason why lullabies are traditional for newborns: They are perfect for lulling a baby to sleep. The high-pitched tones, repetitive verses, and steady rhythm are exactly what many newborns crave. You might even consider recording your voice singing a special song for the times when your baby is away from you.

1. Pick a lullaby you already know or commit to memorizing one new one. You really need only one because this is going to become a direct signal to your baby that it's time to relax.
2. When you sense that she is ready to nod off to sleep, begin singing the lullaby.
3. Repeat the verses, making your voice slower and softer each time. Don't be afraid to sing the lullaby several times in a row. Most lullabies are very short songs designed for this purpose.
4. During the last repeat, stop singing the words and hum the tune until the end, drifting off into silence.
5. If you make this lullaby song your baby's ritual, you might not make it until the second verse before she is asleep.

My Baby's First Book

It's never too early to start a habit of reading to your baby. There is strong evidence to suggest that regularly hearing stories read out loud helps your baby develop a larger vocabulary.

1. Choose a simple board book with high-contrast pictures and just a few words—or even no words at all.
2. Position your baby so he can see the pictures.

Continues on page 13.

DO YOU SPEAK "PARENTESE"?

Chances are that if you regularly talk to your baby throughout the day, you are speaking what's known as Parentese instinctually without being conscious of the change. Babies crave the sound of their parents' voices, and it doesn't seem to matter exactly *what* you are saying to them. What matters more is *how* you say it. Parents who talk to their babies in this manner typically:

- Bend down close to their baby's face (8 to 12 inches away)
- Speak in an exaggerated tone of voice
- Elongate vowels
- Articulate words and phrases clearly
- Shorten sentences
- Vary the vocal sounds, centering mostly on higher pitches
- Use exaggerated facial expressions

Using Parentese is akin to feeding your older baby pureed or softened foods. It makes language easier to digest. The higher-pitched tones make the syllables of your language easier to imitate, as babies have tiny vocal chords themselves. Lengthening the vowels, slowing the rhythm of speech, and enunciating syllables allows babies to home in on the sounds as distinct parts rather than jumbled up together. Using exaggerated facial expressions also connects an emotion or intention to words. For example, raised eyebrows signals that you are asking a question, or a happy smile lets your baby know that something pleasant is about to happen.

3. Read the book out loud in a soft, clear voice. If there are no words, use your own words to describe the pictures. Example: "I see a duck."

Say It, Then Do It

An unexpected new activity that happens very quickly can be an unpleasant experience for a newborn. To help your baby understand that a transition is about to take place, start a habit of giving your baby a heads-up.

1. Before picking your baby up or starting a new activity, tell her what you will do next. For example, if she is wet, you might say "Now I am going to change your diaper."
2. Giving the diaper a little soft pat along with the words is the cue to your baby that you will be walking to the changing table.
3. At first, she will not seem to understand, and you may feel a little awkward, but if you do this consistently, it won't be very long before your baby hears the word "diaper," feels the pat, and knows exactly what will happen. Once that mental connection is made, it will be a relief to her to know what to expect and to have the choice to react to your news.

Social-Emotional Skills

Bonding with your baby does not happen the instant your baby first lies in your arms, when you feed your baby, or when you get up in the middle of the night to change a diaper. There is no one significant moment when a baby becomes firmly attached to a parent. Instead, what we call bonding, or attachment, develops over time from a loving relationship. Every time you gently engage with your baby, you are helping strengthen that bond.

Having an attachment to a caregiver is essential for the developmental health of a baby. Your baby is going to be looking at you and listening to your voice a lot. Your baby wants to know: "Is this new environment safe? How do I drift off to sleep out here in the world? When I'm really hungry, can I count on you to feed me?" Reassurance comes from your loving interactions.

Real-life bonding takes effort and time—and sometimes it's harder and takes longer than you expect. If you find yourself struggling, talk to your doctor or your baby's doctor for support.

Milestones

- **Prefers the human face to all other patterns:** There is nothing a newborn enjoys looking at more than a human face from a close and unobstructed position. You might end up spending a lot more time staring at your baby than you thought possible.
- **Makes eye contact and scans faces for reassurance:** Not only does your baby have a clear preference for looking at your face, but she is also evaluating its meaning. Is there danger out there in the world? Your baby can tell just by looking at your anxious face. By smiling and maintaining eye contact, you are sending the message that it is okay to relax, enjoy the moment, and perhaps even nod off to sleep.
- **Favors the sound of high-pitched human voices:** Parents often instinctually use a high-pitched, singsongy voice, called Parentese (see page 12), to speak to a baby, and there is evidence that babies prefer it. When you use a higher tone, you might notice your baby quieting in response to listen more intently.
- **Turns toward familiar sounds and voices:** The sounds your baby has been hearing for the past nine months are still familiar and comforting. Whether it's a parent's voice, your dog barking, or the phone ringing, you might notice your baby turn toward the sound in interest.
- **Recognizes mother's scent:** Since the last nine months were spent literally growing inside of another person, it's not surprising that that a baby can identify and distinguish this same unique scent in a mother's breast milk immediately after birth.

Games and Activities

Snuggle Scents

The smell of a loved one is incredibly comforting to a newborn. You can use this characteristic to your advantage.

1. Choose a soft, flat item, like a cotton baby blanket or cloth diaper, to imbue with your scent.
2. Snuggle with this item during feeding sessions or while you sleep. It will begin to smell strongly of you. No one else will be able to tell, but your baby will.
3. When you transfer him from your body to another area, such as when having tummy time on the floor or the diaper changing table, lay him on top of the item.
4. When you transfer him from your arms to the arms of a willing relative, or anytime your baby is in the care of another person, you can pass along this item for comfort.
5. The scent will be a point of reference for your baby—a reassuring reminder that you are nearby.

Note: Never leave your baby unattended or sleeping with loose or plush items.

Diaper Talk

Creating a special diaper-changing routine with your baby can make it a more pleasant experience.

1. When your baby needs a new diaper, start by giving her a heads-up. "You are wet. I'm going to change your diaper now."
2. As you complete each step, describe what you are doing as you do it. Make eye contact with her off and on as you proceed.
3. After the dirty diaper is off, your baby is clean, and the new one is on, take a few minutes to interact with her in whatever way feels comfortable—it's a good time for massaging, kissing, and nuzzling.

Good Vibrations

When your baby appears tired or overstimulated—for example, after a long day away from home—it might be time for a good hum.

1. Sit in a rocking chair and place your baby's head on your chest, underneath your chin.
2. Hum in low tones as you rock back and forth.
3. The motion and vibration will likely be soothing.

Notes

This month my baby was especially comforted when I . . .

_____

_____

_____

_____

_____

_____

_____

_____

This month my baby liked to listen to . . .

_____

_____

_____

_____

_____

_____

_____

_____

MONTH

2

Your Baby This Month

Your baby is becoming much more aware of the world, making awake time a little more interactive for the two of you. Life with your baby includes more than meeting basic needs—feeding, diapering, rocking, and sleeping. Your baby starts to anticipate your actions. You see it in new body language and hear it in new vocalizations.

Day and night confusion may ebb by the end of this month if you expose your baby to normal daytime brightness through windows or on shaded walks outside. Fifteen or 16 hours of sleep per day is about the average amount for a two-month-old, but don't expect your baby to sleep through the night. Most babies wake up to eat every three hours or so.

As you settle in to more consistent routines, you might start seeing certain personality traits emerge. While all babies cry to communicate how they feel, some babies are calmer and more easily soothed. One baby might be happy to chill out. Another baby may demand more direct attention, such as being cuddled.

By the end of this month, you may feel like you know how your baby likes to be comforted best. Crying and fussy behavior typically hit their peak midmonth, around six weeks of age. After this point, the worst of it is usually over, and you will likely see fussy behavior steadily decline in frequency and duration in the next couple of months.

Challenges This Month

- **Crying spells:** Around six to eight weeks is when, for most babies, crying has reached its peak and will lessen in the coming months. It can be exhausting trying to keep a baby happy all of the time. Babies have an instinctual urge to cry in order to express emotions. So, yes, there will be crying. Fortunately, babies cannot be spoiled. Pick up and carry your baby as often as you want. Offering those extra snuggles now only helps solidify his sense of trust and security.
- **Routines:** Last month may have seemed like a circus at night with the day and night confusion that is so typical of newborns. Focus on getting into a regular routine that feels good to both you and your baby.
- **Playtime:** Play will still be relatively tame. Stick with simple toys.

Highlights This Month

- **First smile:** Be sure to take photos of those sweet first smiles.
- **First coo:** Your baby is trying to talk to you. As soon as you hear single soft vocal sounds, such as an "ooh" or "aah," mimic them right back.
- **Head control:** Your baby's neck has been getting stronger during these early weeks, leading to more head control.

Motor Skills

It's a time of gentle unfolding and stretching as the newborn reflexes begin to disappear and muscles begin to gain strength. The flailing limbs and tightly curled body of a newborn are a reaction to sensations, driven by the need for closeness and security. Now movement begins to serve a clear purpose. Legs may stretch out and even start to kick. Arms may reach up to bat at objects. Fingers may be discovered with much fascination.

Offer lots of opportunities for your baby to move around freely. A baby who is often confined in a swaddling blanket, swing, stroller, or car seat carrier may not develop the necessary muscle strength for age-appropriate motor skills. It is fine to rely on these occasionally in order to get a quick shower or a bite at a restaurant, among other self-care needs—just take care not to overdo it, because your baby needs to have lots of freedom and a safe space in which to move.

Milestones

- **Newborn reflexes begin disappearing:** Your newborn's reflexes are becoming less and less pronounced with each passing week. For some babies, the grasping reflex and Moro reflex (startling) fade.
- **Movements become more purposeful:** *What are limbs for?* your baby is wondering. With this new awareness, you may see a slight reduction in activity. The flailing decreases and stretches become more meaningful.
- **Lifts up shoulders while lying on stomach:** It may be a slight movement, but if your baby's shoulders are lifting during tummy time, you'll know that the neck muscles are getting stronger.
- **Holds head steady while being held upright:** Your baby may be able to hold a steady head position when held upright for a few seconds, and this ability will continue to develop throughout the next several months. Continue to provide physical support until your baby has full head control. Most babies become adept at this skill by five months old.
- **Keeps head centered and looks straight up while lying down:** You'll likely be noticing the head control developing even when lying down. If you hang a mobile (no strings or ribbons should be longer than seven inches) over the crib, your baby will be delighted at the new ability to look straight up. Remove the mobile when your baby begins to push up on his hands and knees or by five months, whichever comes first.

- **Straightens out legs:** The curled-up legs characteristic of a newborn fades as your baby straightens her legs out and stretches out of the fetal position.
- **Kicks energetically:** Expect a bit of foot action by the end of this month as your baby works to strengthen those leg muscles and develop spatial awareness—the ability to sense where her body is in space. This is setting the stage for rolling over in the next few months.
- **Becomes aware of own hands and brings fingers together:** Discovering the use of one's own hands is cause to celebrate. From here on out, these tiny fingers will begin to unfurl and stretch as the grasping reflex fades. The hands become purposeful tools that help your baby learn about the world. Most babies are able to bring their fingers together by four months.

Games and Activities

It's Better Together

Life is so much nicer when shared with someone you love. Give your baby a real purpose for lifting his head.

1. Find a cozy spot to lie down together on your tummies. This could be on a blanket on your floor or a firm mattress. Make sure it's somewhere comfortable for you.
2. Gaze into your baby's eyes and smile. Give a reassuring back rub while talking about how nice it feels to be together.
3. Place a rattle within 8 to 12 inches of your baby's eyes. Slowly turn or shake it so that it makes a soft sound.
4. Now move the rattle and your body to the other side of your baby's head to encourage him to turn toward you and the sound.
5. Stop when he is ready for a different activity. Most babies don't enjoy long periods of tummy time. A few minutes will do.

Sunrise, Sunset

This activity will help keep your baby's attention focused on your voice as she rises and sets like the sun. Note that this could be a nice morning ritual to incorporate before you go to work.

1. Sit down on the floor with your legs crossed and your back straight. Place a pillow underneath your tailbone if that's more comfortable.
2. Lay your alert baby in front of you on a soft surface, such as a blanket, facing up.

Continues on page 24.

NEWBORN REFLEXES

Rooting reflex: Stroking a cheek elicits a head-turning reflex in the direction of the sensation, followed by an open mouth ready to start sucking. By the third month, when feeding habits have typically been well established, this reflex disappears.

Sucking reflex: Touch the roof of your baby's mouth with a nipple and your baby will begin to suck vigorously. You may notice the sucking reflex fading by the third month.

Tonic neck reflex: Turning your baby's head to the side while lying down causes the arm on that side to stretch out and the opposite arm to bend at the elbow. This reflex is also referred to as the "fencing" position, and it may be evident for about seven months.

Grasping reflex: When you touch the palm of your baby's hand with your finger or another object, the fingers curl up to grasp and hold on tightly. By six months your baby is gaining voluntary hand muscle strength, and grasping is no longer a reflexive response.

Babinski reflex: Stroking the sole of your baby's foot causes the toes to lift up and stretch out. This will remain a reflex for the next two years.

Moro reflex: When your baby hears a loud sound or feels an unexpected movement, you may see this startling reflex. Arms and legs extend, the head is thrust backward, crying may ensue, and then, just as quickly, the arms and legs are pulled back in. This reflex is present for about six months.

Stepping reflex: Placing your baby's feet on the floor causes a lift-step motion that looks quite a bit like your baby is walking. By two or three months, the reflex disappears, and the leg muscles will spend the nextseveral months strengthening themselves for actual purposeful walking.

Continued from page 22.

3. Try to keep your back straight as you bend down until you are about 8 to 12 inches away from her face and smile at her to capture her attention and focus.
4. So that your baby can anticipate what is coming, say, "Are you ready to be the sun?"
5. Scoop your hands under her head and your forearms under her bottom, so that you're securely supporting her in a position that allows you to comfortably lift her up to your shoulder.
6. Still keeping your back straight, lift your baby up toward your shoulder while you sing a scale—do-re-mi-fa-so-la-ti-do—starting with a lower pitch and progressively going up to a higher pitch.
7. When you get to the top of the scale, sing a scale again, this time with your pitch starting high and progressively getting lower—do-ti-la-so-fa-mi-re-do. As you sing, lower your baby back down.
8. Repeat as often as you and your baby are enjoying this game.

A Gooooood Stretch

Your baby will likely enjoy this gentle leg stretch.

1. Lean down over your baby's face and give a big smile to capture his focus and attention.
2. Now hold one foot in each hand and gently kiss your baby's toes.
3. Gently lift your baby's legs up and inward toward his belly. Then gently pull his feet in the opposite direction, toward you. During the stretch, coo, saying, "Ooh, ahh . . . That feels gooood!"
4. You can stroke your baby's legs from hip to toe, massaging the thighs and calves to encourage this brief stretch.

Bell and Ribbon

As your baby begins to make the connection between the sound of a bell ringing and her hand hitting it or her foot kicking it, she's starting to understand the concept of cause and effect.

1. Securely knot or sew a jingle bell that's at least 1.25 inches in diameter to a ribbon that's no more than seven inches long.
2. Position your baby on her back so she can look straight up.

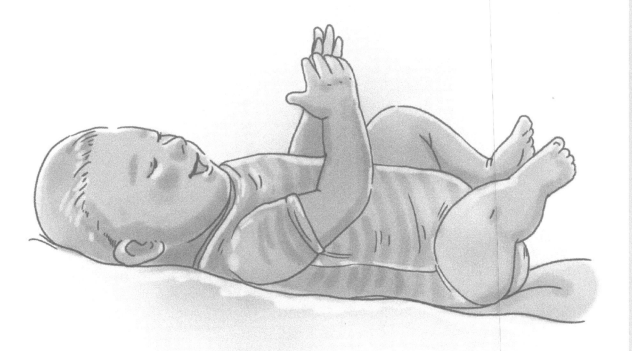

3. Hold the ribbon so the bell is about 12 inches above her upper chest and lightly jingle it to capture her attention.

4. Lower the bell so your baby can reach it with her hands. As her motor skills improve, she will try to swipe the bell with her fists. You can also hold it above her feet when she is learning to kick.

5. When your baby is ready to change activities, always put away the ribbon and bell where she can't reach it. Never leave your baby unattended with them.

Sensory Development

The differences between the first and second months are subtle but important. Your baby's vision, while slow to develop, is steadily improving. Bright colors become a point of interest, as do more complex patterns. Black-and-white images remain intriguing, but you might notice that your baby is drawn to vibrant colors, such as fire-engine red or royal blue. Slowly moving objects continue to appeal to your baby, and you may notice an increase in visual tracking during playtime. When offering objects for viewing, keep them at close range, as distance vision has still not developed farther than about 10 inches away.

Physical contact and reassuring sounds are essential for your baby. The skin, highly sensitized, is constantly seeking a reassuring touch. Brief massages can feel pleasantly stimulating, but even simply being held while awake or sleeping is immensely gratifying. Your baby is learning what it feels like to be a person who is loved by another, and you are setting the stage now for healthy relationships in the future.

Milestones

- **Focuses on objects moving across field of vision:** Your baby's ability to track slowly moving objects is much improved. Mobiles are even more fascinating, and so are your lips as you speak.
- **Prefers to look at more complex patterns:** Your baby's eyes are extra attuned to complex patterns. The simple, bold patterns that were so appealing last month are less interesting, and your baby favors more detailed images.
- **Prefers colorful patterns:** Although your baby's favorite thing to look at is still primarily your face, it's time to bring some vibrant colors into your baby's close visual range.
- **Unexpected movements and noises are still startling:** Your little one is still easily unnerved by unexpected noises. You may see the startling reflex with flailing limbs occasionally. Reassuring your baby with soothing tones and physical contact helps.
- **Enjoys skin massages:** The skin is the largest organ of the human body, and your baby is sensitive to any contact point. Most babies this age enjoy the sensation of a gentle massage now and then, along with all the regular kisses and hugs.

Games and Activities

Color Splash

The ability to see brighter colors can make a world of difference to your baby now.

1. Look for objects around the house with bright colors for your baby to look at, such as a toy, piece of artwork, or mobile.
2. Prepare her for the activity by saying, "I'd like to show you some bright colors."
3. Find a position where she can see the colorful object. If you have a toy, for example, hold her in your lap. To see a securely hung piece of artwork or mobile, hold her over your shoulder.
4. Allow your baby to gaze at the colors as long as desired.

Happy Feet

Foot massages can be soothing or stimulating depending on your baby's mood.

1. Sit down on a blanket on the floor. Place your baby in front of you facing up.
2. Bend down, make eye contact, and say, "I would like to feel your feet. Where are those feet?"
3. Starting with the crown of his head, lightly trail your fingers down the sides of his body until you reach his feet.
4. Lift up a leg with one hand and use your index finger to lightly tap the bottom of the foot for a few seconds. Switch to the other side.
5. Now lift up both legs and use the pads of your thumbs to rub figure eights on the bottoms of your baby's feet. After one to two minutes of rubbing, kiss each foot to end the session.

Did You Hear That?

Your baby's new awareness of the world around her can be confusing. Help her understand what is scary and what is not.

1. When your baby startles or cries in reaction to a loud noise, explain the source of the sound.
2. Ask her, "Did you hear that noise?"
3. Explain what the noise is. For example, say, "That was the washing machine beeping. It won't hurt you. It's letting us know that our clothes are finished being washed." If possible, take her over to the object that made the sound to show that there is no danger.

The Comet

Engage your baby's improving eye-tracking ability with a bit of playtime.

1. Lay your baby faceup on a blanket on the floor during an alert, wakeful period.
2. Whisper animatedly, "Watch. Here comes a comet."
3. Shake a soft rattle on one side of your baby's head, and then slowly move it across his range of vision (still 8 to 12 inches away) to the other side.
4. End the comet's path with another rattling sound.

Language and Mental Development

Have you heard any cute little *oohing* and *aahing* from your baby yet? If not, they will be coming soon. Last month, your baby learned that crying is an effective method to announce that it's time to eat or express displeasure with a wet diaper. She's now starting to understand that you are also able to offer other forms of emotional support. As your baby learns to announce moods and needs with other types of vocalizations, such as cooing and gurgling, life calms down considerably. Talking back reinforces the idea that these are valid ways to get your attention.

Your baby is also internalizing your habits and daily routines. For example, when you take your baby to the place where you normally change a diaper, you might notice your baby showing extra energy with a focused gaze toward your face and wiggling legs. When you take out the pillow that you use for feeding, your baby may relax and go completely still, waiting for the sweet taste of milk. Simple soothing techniques, such as snuggling, dancing, and humming, help your baby learn that it's okay to relax.

Milestones

- **Crying reaches its peak:** Crying remains your baby's primary attention-getting method, typically peaking around six to eight weeks.
- **Watches parents' lips move:** Your baby may wonder, "How do my parents make that noise? Can I make it, too?" He may start to imitate you by moving his lips. When being held in your arms, 8 to 12 inches is the perfect distance to watch your lips.

- **May begin to coo and gurgle:** Your baby may be exploring vocalizations and indicating happiness with soft single-vowel sounds. Babies are not able to swallow saliva for about a year, so when it pools in the back of the throat, you hear a gurgle.
- **Recognizes familiar objects:** Objects within your baby's field of vision that he sees often become more recognizable.
- **Anticipates familiar routines:** As you interact with your baby, daily habits are solidifying into a comfortable routine.

Games and Activities

Do You Want to Know a Secret?

You and your baby are developing a relationship based on trust and intimate communication. The more you talk to him, the more he tries to talk to you, too.

1. As you are going about your daily activities, lean in closely and whisper about what you like or dislike and why.
2. When out and about or while with other people, take a moment now and then to whisper in his ear. Even a simple "I love you" can make him feel more secure.

Dance Party

This bit of exercise can soothe your baby and give you a little endorphin rush. It can also be a great way to reconnect if you have been apart during the day.

1. Clear a space to dance where you won't trip on anything.
2. Put on some music with a fast, pumping beat. Make sure the volume is not too loud.
3. Rock out to the rhythm with your baby securely in your arms or on your chest in a baby carrier.

The Story of You

You have a rapt audience. Try out some storytelling.

1. Look into your baby's eyes and lean in closely to get focused attention. Your baby may begin looking at your lips as soon as you start talking.
2. Now tell your baby the story of her birth. Explain how she grew inside of you and how she was born.
3. Emphasize over and over how much she is loved and how much she has grown.

Social-Emotional Skills

The act of expressing our emotions to a loved one and feeling understood and accepted in return is a basic human need. Even now, your infant is making progress toward social intimacy and give-and-take relationships. Every time you use physical touch to soothe your baby or smile to convey your love and joy of being with your baby, you are teaching lifelong social skills and helping her make the connection between emotion and action.

It's a bit on the early side, but sometime this month, your baby might begin to intentionally smile. It could mean, "I see you," "I'm enjoying this moment," or even "I can't wait to see what's coming next." Even if your baby isn't smiling quite yet, your face is becoming familiar and preferred, associated with your speaking voice, your favorite snuggling positions, and the songs you sing.

Milestones

- **Recognizes parents' faces:** All that time gazing into your newborn's eyes has imprinted your facial features in his mind. Now when you're nearby, your baby recognizes you visually as well as by your smell.
- **Is soothed and reassured by parents' touch:** Your baby may still be very fussy. Laying a hand on a part of your baby's body or picking your baby up at the first whimper can calm her and prevent crying.
- **May smile in response to parents' smiles:** The reflex smile transforms into a real smile this month or maybe sometime in the next month. Smiling back and forth in imitation is a fun game for you and your baby once this ability begins.
- **May smile spontaneously to express pleasure:** It's a bit on the early side for your baby to show contentment through a facial expression, but it is the natural next step after an imitating smile. Familiar objects or routines that she enjoys may bring out that first expression of happiness. Be on the lookout for this from now through the third month.

Games and Activities

Good Morning, Baby!

Make greeting the new day part of your morning routine. This is a great way to connect before you leave for work.

1. Sit down on a flat surface. Keep your legs together and bend your knees. Have your baby sit facing you on your lap, supported by your upper legs. Smile at him.
2. Hold your baby's hands and, if he is willing, gently lift them up toward the sky. Say, "Good morning!" Keep the stretch brief.
3. Tell your baby the day's itinerary, whether you're going to be together or apart. "Today we're going to . . ."

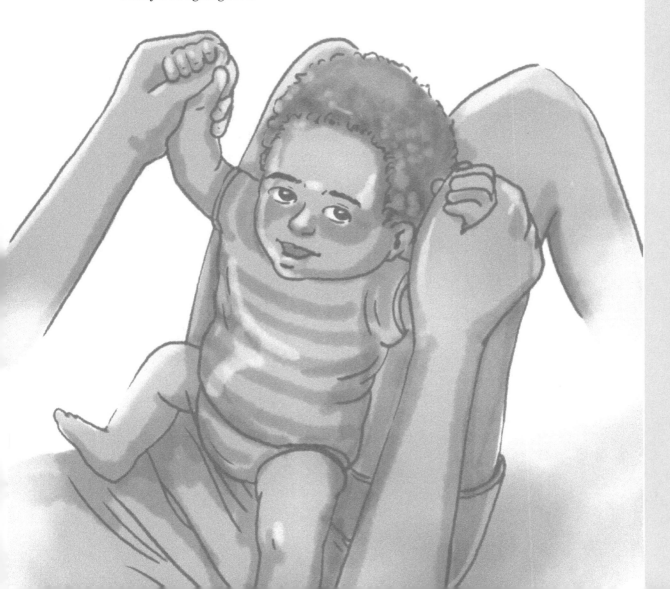

Kissy Face

Express your love with this kissing game and encourage a social smile.

1. Start at the top of her face and work your way down. Say, "I love your forehead!"
2. Follow the words with a kiss right on her forehead and a big smile.
3. Keep playing this game as you move down her face. You might then kiss her eyelids, nose, cheeks, ears, and chin. Your baby might even begin cooing and smiling in response if you wait long enough between kisses.

Come Along with Me

Whether during the day, on weekends, or in the evenings, take a little companion along as you do your chores, narrating your actions along the way. The extra physical contact will be reassuring.

1. Tell your baby what activity you are about to do and why you're going to do it. For example, "It's time for me to do the laundry because our clothes are dirty."
2. Ask your baby to come with you, in your arms or in a baby carrier. For example, "Would you like to come help me? Let's go see the washing machine."
3. Talk about what you're doing as you do it. For example, "Now I'm putting the dirty clothes in. There they go into the washer. I'm pushing this button to fill it with water."

THAT FIRST SMILE

During the first month and a half, your baby's mouth twitching up at the corners is probably a reflex, a movement practiced even in the womb. A reflex smile occurs at random times and has no social context. Just as the muscles of the legs or arms quiver without overt purpose, so do your baby's facial muscles.

Typically, sometime in the second or third month, this reflex disappears and the "social smile" appears. In parenting, that first smile is a game changer, and most parents are thrilled to see it. If your baby looks at your smiling face, gazes into your eyes, and gives you a gummy grin and then later does it again, you know it's for real. It will still be some time, though, before that smile is used with intention to convey happiness.

Notes

Some of the secrets I told my baby were . . .

This month my baby and I danced to these songs:

MONTH

3

Your Baby This Month

Your little caterpillar has started to morph into a social butterfly interested in engaging playfully with you. She is likely to greet you with intense gazes, smiles, and vocalizations. She is starting to learn that you can be trusted to address her needs, whether hunger or a diaper change. As your baby's ability to communicate develops, the need to use crying to let you know she needs something decreases. Keep being responsive and speaking Parentese. By the end of this month, your baby will likely coo back to you and wiggle around excitedly when you make funny noises.

Playtime is getting a lot more fun and interactive. Most babies are getting a lot better at holding their heads up, and those abdominal and limb muscles are likely being put to good use. Offer toys for tasting and shaking, and hold a toy down low toward her feet for her to kick.

Life may be feeling a little more fun, but remember—babies don't need to be stimulated constantly. Simple, isolated experiences are the best. Downtime is important, and your baby will let you know that it's time for a little quiet by turning away or closing her eyes. Follow her lead.

Challenges This Month

- **Feeding changes:** Your baby may suddenly change feeding patterns, which can be surprising, especially for breastfeeding mothers. All of a sudden, your baby may finish a nursing session in 5 to 10 minutes—he might just be that efficient.
- **Getting your baby to sleep:** Does your baby seem to need you to nod off to sleep for a nap or at bedtime? You may have heard or read advice suggesting that you put your baby to bed while awake, not while being rocked or fed—and that may work for some babies. For others, though, it may have the opposite effect, and you may end up with an unhappy, sleep-deprived baby. There is nothing wrong with soothing your baby to sleep at this stage, and it will not impact her ability to self-soothe when she's a bit older. Just do what feels right and works for your family for now.
- **Dealing with demands:** You know your baby's crying means your attention is needed. It's just that sometimes he has to wait a moment while you do what you need to do. Is that okay? Absolutely! Your needs are important, too. While it is important that you tend to him when you hear distress, a little fussing for a few minutes might be necessary. You can talk to your baby to tell him to wait just a minute and you'll be right there. And then, when you're ready to pick him up again, make sure to thank him for waiting. If you find yourself getting overly frustrated or angry because your child is crying for a long period of time, put your baby in a safe place, like the crib, and take a break to calm yourself.

Highlights This Month

- **More confidence:** You might be feeling a burst of pride. You and your baby are on the verge of passing from the newborn period into infancy.
- **Time for some toys:** Since your baby's motor skills are taking a big leap, toys are suddenly a lot more fun. You don't need many, though, just a handful with a range of textures and shapes for your child to explore.
- **Self-entertainment:** What a delight it is when you realize that your baby is able to entertain herself with a toy for a few minutes.

Motor Skills

Your baby will be bursting with activity, although most of it is happening in small, concentrated muscle-strengthening exercises, such as batting at objects, grasping and shaking toys, and lifting up during tummy time. This drive to become more physically adept makes playtime more interactive for both of you. You'll want to make plenty of time for your baby to hang out in his favorite movement area on the floor.

Gravity is becoming a point of interest as well. Whether lying down on his back or sitting in your lap, your baby will experiment with foot and leg movements—actions that prepare him to roll over. You'll notice his feet tapping around to find places to push off. If you hold your baby up, he will likely bear some weight. Rolling over may be in the near future if he hasn't managed to flip over already.

Milestones

- **Holds head steady for longer periods:** Your baby may be able to hold a steady head position when held or in a supported seated position, and this ability continues to develop throughout the next several months. Make sure to provide physical support until your baby has full head control. Most babies become adept at this skill by five months old.
- **Improved upper body strength:** Your baby might be becoming adept at raising his head and chest and using his arms to lift up when lying on his stomach. Tummy time becomes more enjoyable for your baby as the neck muscles become strong enough for him to lift his head and look around. Offer plenty of opportunities for practice by giving your baby interesting objects to look at.
- **Stretching legs and kicking more vigorously:** Expect your baby to express excitement through this urge to stretch and kick. By moving her feet and legs around when lying on her stomach or back, your baby is exploring the way her body moves through space as part of preparing to roll over.
- **Pushes down with legs and feet:** When you hold your baby over a firm surface, you may notice that his legs bear weight and bounce. It is too early for babies to stand on their own, but it's not too early to explore the effects of gravity and counter it with stronger legs.
- **Opens and closes hands:** How nice it is to be able to open one's hands to receive and hold on to an object. Your baby's fingers practice this motion even when there is no toy around: She brings them up to eye level to play with. Most babies can bring their fingers together by four months old.

- **Grasping, shaking, and swiping with the hands:** Your baby reaches out to interact with objects. Offer a variety of differently shaped and textured objects for him to grasp, shake, and take a swipe at.

Games and Activities

Splashy Kicks

Kicking bathwater strengthens your baby's legs and shows another example of cause and effect when the water splashes.

1. Fill your bathtub with just a few inches of water and make sure that the ambient temperature is comfortable. Allow your baby to watch this process so that she is able to anticipate the event.
2. Lower your baby into the tub gently so she's on her back with a folded towel for extra comfort, or sit behind her with her resting against your belly. Make sure her head is not submerged in the water.
3. Your baby may start to kick right away, but if she does not, you may also lift her legs up and show her how to splash.

Note: Never leave your baby unattended near water.

Baby Cakes

Mix different sounds by chanting a rhyme while shaking two rattles.

1. Lay your baby on his back and sit in front of him.
2. Offer two rattles or jingling toys to your baby. Encourage him to grasp them by lightly touching each palm with a toy. If your baby is not interested, you may shake the rattles yourself.
3. Now chant the Baby Cakes rhyme as you do the accompanying actions.

Shake, shake, shake	(help your baby shake both rattles in rhythm)
I'm going to make you a cake	(keep shaking)
Flour	(shake rattle on right side)
Butter	(shake rattle on left side)
Mix it all together	(rub your baby's belly)
Put it in the oven, and	(pat your baby's belly)
Eat it up!	(kiss and pretend to eat your baby's belly)

TIPS FOR INTRODUCING
TOYS AND ACTIVITIES

When introducing toys or other hands-on activities to your baby, gauge her reaction. She may bubble with excitement or turn away disinterested. Follow her cues. Some of these tips for trying something new will become more important as your child gets older, but they're good to keep in mind from the early months.

Gain consent first. Instead of directly placing an object into your child's hands, get her attention and ask first. Cradle the object in your palms and hold it out in front of you to be taken or place it nearby. This leaves the choice up to your child. Even though it may seem like this doesn't matter at such a young age, you're modeling respect.

Slow down your movements. Got it? Great. Now slow them down even further. Allow your baby's eyes the time needed to fully appreciate the movements you are making as you demonstrate the properties of the toy or activity.

Respect your child's concentration. No doubt your baby is hungry for the chance to communicate with you, but there is also a time and place for silence. If your baby is beginning to focus on an object, don't feel like you need to say anything. Appreciate this moment of hard work and keep distractions to a minimum. When your baby looks up at you again, you'll know it's time to reengage.

Hang back. Give your baby ample opportunity to explore a new object on her own. This becomes increasingly important as your baby's motor skills develop and she plays more independently. It's okay if there's some frustration as your baby works through something. By not jumping to her rescue and assisting her to the end goal too quickly, you're giving her the chance to learn to persevere and enjoy the satisfaction of her work. If she's genuinely distressed, comfort her and do something else.

Learn step-by-step. As activities become more complex through the months, practice just one small part of an activity at a time and later put the parts together. This way your baby can gain confidence before moving on to the next step. This also works with toys that have multiple parts, such as a set of blocks. Start with one object at a time, then add more.

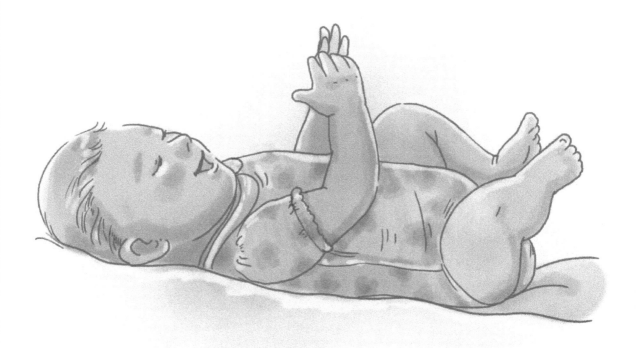

Springing Ring

A version of batting practice lets your baby attempt some new tricks.

1. Securely attach a strong, stretchy cord no longer than seven inches to a ring-shaped toy.
2. Lay your baby on her back on a soft surface, such as a mat.
3. Show your baby how the toy springs back and bounces in the air if you pull and then release it.
4. Hold it over her and give her a chance to try to grasp and shake it, but don't worry if she just wants to bat it.

Note: Before use, always check the cord to make sure it is securely attached to the toy, and always put it away as soon as you're done. Never leave your baby unattended with a cord.

Sensory Development

Your baby's sense of sight continues to advance. Objects and people who are farther away become more recognizable, although he continues to watch your face intently while playing or feeding.

Sounds, tastes, and smells all continue to interest your baby. The differences between loud and soft, sweet and sour, and floral and spicy all become more and more distinguishable. Babies can easily detect the difference between their own mother's milk and that of another mother or between different kinds of formula, and they definitely have preferences. Breastfeeding mothers may note that the flavors consumed in food, especially those of cruciferous vegetables or strong spices, do pass through into the breast milk. A baby may react with surprise, delight, or dismay if her mother's diet has changed suddenly.

Milestones

- **Focusing and tracking abilities continue to improve:** Your baby tracks moving objects that pass through his visual range more precisely. By this point, most babies are no longer crossing their eyes. Both eyes can be turned inward to focus on an object in the foreground.
- **Distance vision develops:** Your baby can also focus at longer distances now and may react when passing by a familiar object or person.
- **Starts using hands and eyes in coordination:** Such a skill may seem like no big deal to us as adults, but to your baby, the ability to manipulate a toy and look at it at the same time opens up a whole new world of exploration.
- **Turns head toward direction of sound:** Noises may be a little less scary as familiar sounds provoke interest rather than anxiety. Your baby is learning that the world is comfortable and predictable.
- **Distinguishes between different colors, tastes, and smells:** The colors of the rainbow are appearing especially bright now. You may also notice that your baby has stronger likes and dislikes when it comes to smells and tastes, which can affect feeding.

Games and Activities

My Family Book

Faces are fascinating to three-month-olds, especially those of family members. Don't forget to add your own face to the book.

1. Create a "My Family" book by taking face-only photos of family members and putting them into a premade photo album or by pasting them into a repurposed baby board book.
2. Lie down next to your baby in a comfortable position.
3. Show your baby each family member's face, saying the name of that person. For example, "This is Grandma."
4. Add a little extra information about each person while you read. For example, "Grandma loves you very much. She comes to our house and holds you."
5. Place the book in a basket or on a shelf in your baby's play area. Read the book often, and your baby will memorize those facial features.

Nuzzle Dance

Snuggling while standing up feels so good. You can make a game out of it, too.

1. Stand up and hold your baby vertically with his head on your shoulder so that you are face-to-face.
2. Make sure that you are in an area where you have room to move without worrying about tripping.
3. Now say the Nuzzle Dance rhyme below in a singsong voice with the accompanying actions.

Eye to eye	(lean in closely)
And nose to nose	(touch your nose to baby's nose)
Round and round my baby goes.	(spin slowly one turn)

4. Repeat the game if desired.

Note: Spinning too quickly is unpleasant and disorienting to babies at this age, so keep it slow.

Patta Game

"Pat-A-Cake" is a classic baby game that helps to develop hand-eye coordination.

1. Lay your baby down on a soft blanket in front of you while she's in a playful mood.
2. Gently take both of her forearms in your hands and clap her hands together while you chant this rhyme. Slow down toward the end.

Patta in the morning	(clap rhythmically at a moderate speed)
Patta through the night	
Patta patta in your bed	
And now turn off the light	(clap slower and slower)
Good night!	(stop clapping)

Language and Mental Development

Your baby's language and mental development can be summed up with the acronym EIR: Experimentation, Imitation, and Repetition. During the past two months, your baby has been watching and listening to you intently to make connections between the sounds you make and the actions you take. Now he is starting to connect the dots and try these sounds himself.

It may not sound like much at first. Your baby's first coo, that single-vowel "aah" or "ooh" sound, will be brief and hesitant, an experiment to see how it feels in the mouth and if it can be replicated. He will do it again and again sometimes to see if you notice and react.

If you do, this first back-and-forth linguistic adventure becomes intellectually stimulating, and your baby actively imitates any and all of the sounds you make, including coos, squeals, and growls.

Milestones

- **Squeals, growls, and coos:** Oh, the funny sounds your baby can make to experiment with language. As she gets older, you will be hearing quite the variety. By the end of this month, most babies are cooing. Some may also be growling and squealing.
- **Laughs out loud:** It's on the early side for belly laughs, but you may start hearing a chuckle when you play silly games, make interesting sounds, or gently tickle.
- **Razzing:** Sometime around now or in the next few months, your baby may make a wet razzing sound by buzzing together the lips and tongue and blowing air. Fair warning: This funny sound might make you laugh, which will make your baby want to do it again.
- **Able to entertain self for brief periods:** There's no way to know when or for how long a baby will be able to entertain himself, but some babies begin enjoying brief self-directed play with toys this month. This partly depends on your baby's temperament and current mood.

Games and Activities

Face Playtime

This game is adapted from a traditional nursery rhyme and allows for plenty of face-to-face interaction.

1. Lay your baby down on his back while you lean over his face, capturing his gaze.
2. Now say these words with the accompanying touches on your baby's face.

Knock on the door	(lightly knock on forehead)
Peep in	(touch one eyebrow, then the other)
Lift the latch	(touch the tip of the nose)
Walk in	(walk your two fingers just under lips)
There's a chair	(tap left cheek)
Sit right there	(tap right cheek)
How do you do?	(gently hold chin and move jaw up and down)
Good afternoon!	

Buzzy Bee

Try to make your baby laugh with an unexpected tickle.

1. In a comfortable space, lie down on your back side by side with your baby.
2. Raise your outer hand up in the air, above your heads.
3. Make a buzzing sound and fly your hand around through the air. Keep your hand close enough and slow enough for your baby to focus. *Bzz, bzz, bzz.*
4. For the final act, buzz the bee down to your baby's belly and tickle.

Puppet Babble Play

If your baby is making vocalizations, like babbling, razzing, squealing, cooing, and gurgling, you are likely doing a lot of imitation play already. Make it different this time with a puppet doing the babbling.

1. Lean back in a chair or on your couch with your knees bent. Now sit your baby in your lap facing you and get comfortable with your legs supporting him.
2. Hold a puppet or toy animal between you and your baby. Dance the puppet around a bit, saying hello and making funny noises.
3. Allow your baby several seconds of silence between noises to give him a chance to imitate the noise: He may need the mental processing time.

Social-Emotional Skills

The best toys in the world to your baby are not physical objects but the people he interacts with. Your baby's more highly developed visual acuity, senses, and language skills now combine to help facilitate deeper and more engaging human interaction. You may find that he is interested in gazing at your face and other people's faces for longer and longer periods of time. Playtime may be suddenly a lot more enjoyable than before, and he may now seek out what was previously overstimulating.

Your face and voice are constantly being evaluated, but this time he is not just looking to see whether a situation is a safe or scary one but to learn what facial expressions and tones are associated with different emotional states.

As your baby learns from you and experiments with social cues, it should be easier to understand what he is feeling, as joy and sadness are more apparent in his facial expressions. Body language can give you a lot of information about whether he is enjoying playtime or would rather do something else.

Milestones

- **Enjoys playing with others:** Since stranger anxiety typically has not set in yet, your baby may thoroughly enjoy playing with other people. When playtime is over, you may hear a bit of fussing in protest.
- **Uses facial expressions and body language:** Your baby is becoming more communicative and expressive. You might notice signs of joy or displeasure at familiar and new faces and in your daily routines. Moving arms and kicking legs may indicate excitement. A crinkled nose or squirming may show discontent.
- **Maintains eye contact for longer periods:** Your baby is starting to understand that giving visual attention to someone can produce results. The intensity of your baby's gaze increases and lengthens when trying to get your attention.
- **Anticipates daily routines:** Is it time for a new diaper? Your baby understands now what will likely happen when you lean down and feel his bottom for wetness. He may react with intense eye contact, stillness, waving limbs, or even squirming when you lean down to begin a common daily action like diapering, feeding, or getting ready for bedtime.
- **Reacts more dramatically to your voice:** Your baby has always preferred the sound of your voice over others', but now his response is more intense. When you use a soothing tone, his body may relax. When you speak, even if it's across the room, he may respond with a smile.

Games and Activities

The Getcha Game

Anticipation is the name of the game, as most babies this age love being "caught."

1. Lay your baby on her back while you sit in front of her. Make sure she is in a playful mood.
2. In a slow voice that rises higher and higher in pitch, tell her that you are going to get a body part. For example, "I'm gonna get your . . . nose!"
3. Give a little tickle or kiss on each body part that you "get."

Can't Stop Staring at You

It's meditation for you, and it's eye contact practice for your baby.

1. While your baby is in a calm, alert state, hold him in a cradling position. If you are breastfeeding, this time might be ideal. An alternate pose is sitting your baby in your lap facing you while your knees are bent.
2. Say, "I love you" to initiate eye contact.
3. When your baby looks at you, don't look away. Smile and gaze back intently. Breathe deeply and regularly and stay very still while maintaining eye contact.
4. Hold the gaze until eye contact is broken by your baby. Never pull his face back around to look at you again. By acknowledging your baby's control in this social situation, you are conveying respect.

Peekaboo

Surprise your baby with your face, and you might get a big smile.

1. Lay your baby on her back while you sit in front. Make sure she is in a playful mood.
2. Cover your face with your hands, and then quickly part them, saying, "Peekaboo!"
3. Try covering your face with some other simple props, such as a piece of paper or a book.

I'm Always Here for You

Do you hear a coo for attention? Go right over and see what your baby might need. This game strengthens your relationship by letting him know you're there when needed—even if it's just for playtime.

1. When you hear a coo, tell your baby you are always there if needed.
2. Ask him if he needs various things and try them out. For example, ask "Do you need a hug?" and then if he is receptive, hug him.
3. If you are pretty certain he has all his basic needs met and really just wants your attention, don't be afraid to get silly. For example, ask "Do you need a wiggle on your pinkie toe?" or "Do you need a kiss on your left ear?"

Notes

Some books I read to my baby this month were . . .

A game my baby enjoyed this month was . . .

MONTH

4

Your Baby This Month

Every week that passes allows you to get to know your baby's unique qualities better and better. Daily routines are not just familiar, they are anticipated and comforting. It seems like everywhere you go, even places you personally find lackluster, there is somehow something new and fascinating for your baby to investigate. You might find yourself exploring your home and outdoor environment in an entirely different way. Everything that can be safely sucked on or manipulated by your baby's little fingers is a potential toy.

By now the newborn reflexes that allowed your baby to learn to feed effectively have faded. He knows how to tell you when it's time to eat and assumes the best position with purposeful determination. You can breathe easily, knowing that he knows what to do and how to ask for it.

Your baby will still cry when overtired or dissatisfied or when your assistance is otherwise needed, but the tears will typically be shorter-lived because he knows by now that you can be trusted to help. Socthing techniques will likely feel more automatic to you as well. In the past three months, you have learned his preferred calming techniques, and it requires less mental energy on your part to offer them.

Challenges This Month

- **Sleep regressions:** It's not you or your bedtime routine, it's just your baby. These disruptions in sleep may include going to sleep earlier or later than usual, waking up more often to feed, or fussing for much longer before settling down.
- **Distraction:** Like the puppy that sees a squirrel and darts away, your baby's response to sounds and movement is fast and furious. Those more attuned senses mean that she is apt to get distracted during routine activities. This is not usually a problem unless you are trying to have a calm feeding session. Turning away may not mean that your baby is finished. If it happens frequently, feeding in a less stimulating environment may help.
- **Frustration:** When babies are trying to perform new physical feats, such as reaching a toy during tummy time or rolling over, you may hear some fussing. Responding to your baby's cries is still important, but a bit of frustration is normal and can help provide the motivation she needs to refine these gross motor skills. Don't jump in too soon to solve the problem.

Highlights This Month

- **Meaningful conversations:** The art of conversing with another human being is a mystery to solve. When you speak, if you give your baby a bit of response time, you may find that she enjoys cooing or babbling back to you. Feel free to converse about anything. She won't care what you're talking about, but she will love the conversation.
- **Ready to roll:** Some babies actively twist and turn to try to roll over. When it finally happens, it can be a very exciting and surprising moment for both of you.
- **Laughter:** Your giggling infant appreciates silly voices and animated facial expressions. Be prepared to repeat the games that get the biggest laughs—over and over. Babies love repetition.

Motor Skills

You are likely to see your baby's full torso, including back and abdominal muscles, engaged to the fullest, straining upward and outward. No longer satisfied to simply lie down and be entertained, he has a full agenda: learn to push up, reach and grab items of interest, and roll over.

Some babies will be well into rolling already, but yours may still be working on this milestone or skipping it altogether, and that is perfectly okay. To encourage this skill, notice when he begins to rock back and forth, then hold an interesting object just out of reach on one side. Most babies find rolling from front to back a bit easier. Rolling from a faceup position takes more effort. There are no special exercises you need to do with him. In fact, simply making time and space for freedom of movement with minimum distractions is the best thing you can do.

Milestones

- **Pushes up on elbows and hands:** These mini pushups during tummy time allow your baby to look around to see all of the interesting things in his play space. A few toys, a colorful book, and a baby-safe mirror nearby will be especially enticing. Some may even use their arms to scoot around.
- **Sits supported:** There is no need to practice the sitting position or prop up your baby. Instead, you will likely naturally find yourself nestling him comfortably in your lap while you read stories or explore objects together. You will notice more head control in general, and if you give him enough freedom and space to learn how to scrunch, push, and pivot his body around, sometime soon you will find your baby suddenly able to sit up for brief moments, discovering this new ability all on his own.
- **Rocks and reaches:** Whether your baby is already rolling over or is not quite there yet, you might be noticing a lot of focused twisting, rocking, and reaching, which strengthens muscles. This concentrated effort is in preparation for bigger, more powerful motor movements such as rolling from back to front, scooting, and eventually crawling.
- **Bounces on feet:** Your baby may enjoy bearing weight on her legs and bouncing. If she grabs your hands and pulls herself up, this is a natural and healthy activity for her to engage in. No need for baby jumpers, exersaucers, walkers, and activity centers. Your baby knows intuitively what exact movements are most helpful.
- **Plays with toes:** Most babies this age will, with quite some delight, discover their toes and even be able to taste them. This allows for a dual sensory input experience that is utterly fascinating, so enjoy this bit of cuteness while it lasts.

Games and Activities

I See Me

Babies love pushing up to look in mirrors—even though they don't yet comprehend that they're seeing themselves.

1. Securely install a large unbreakable mirror next to your baby's primary movement area, low enough that she can look at it from the floor, or use a mirror that's already installed in your home.
2. Position yourself and your baby so that you can look in the mirror together. Peering at your reflections, do whatever entertains your baby—make funny faces, touch your nose, or wave a hand.

This Little Duckling

Your baby may already be interested in exploring her toes, making it just the right time for a little toe play that also reminds her about the people in her life.

1. Tell your baby you would like to play a game with her toes. A nice beginning to this game is a kiss on the foot.
2. Now, holding one foot gently in your palm with one hand, use your index finger and thumb to wiggle each toe in succession while you say this rhyme in a high-pitched, exaggerated tone of voice. In the last line, fill in your name or the name of someone in your baby's life: Mommy, Daddy, Grandma.
3. Start with the biggest toe and end with the pinkie toe.
4. You can finish this game with another kiss or a tickle.
5. Repeat this game with different names in the last line.

> *This little duckling waddled to the door.*
> *This little duckling plopped on the floor.*
> *This little duckling stayed in to play.*
> *This little duckling ran away.*
> *This little duckling said, "Quackie, quack! I'm waiting for [person's name]*
> *to come back!"*

The Good Kind of Frustration

When your baby is determined and frustrated when trying to reach a desired object, the motivation to move and get over there is very strong.

1. While your baby is lying on her back or tummy, put a toy nearby but not within arm's reach.
2. Play with the toy for a bit yourself, and then leave it where it is and move to the side, away from the toy. Calmly and quietly watch to see what happens.
3. If your baby begins to rock or reach toward the toy but is still unable to obtain it, don't jump in right away to hand the toy over. A little fussing might be an expression of emotion that means "I'm working hard right now to reach that thing I want." Validate and respect that emotion, telling her that you can see that she is working hard.
4. If your baby cries in full-out unhappiness, it is perfectly okay to either assist or change activities and try it again another time.

Sensory Development

As a newborn, the rooting reflex and sucking reflex of the mouth allowed your baby to find the source of nourishment and effectively feed. Those reflexes have disappeared, but the desire to find something to put in the mouth has not diminished. Mouthing objects is now the primary method by which your baby explores and learns about the physical properties of toys and other objects. Touching and exploring with fingers will happen later, when fine motor skills develop.

Everything and anything in your baby's reach will end up in his mouth for tasting. No matter how dirty, and no matter how much of a choking hazard or how otherwise inappropriate it is, he will attempt to suck or chew on it. Have on hand age-appropriate toys that are safe for your curious child to put in the mouth and explore, and be extra vigilant about keeping anything that's a choking hazard out of reach (see page 59).

Milestones

- **Mouths objects:** By sucking, chewing, and exploring objects with the tongue, your baby learns a lot about the shape, size, and texture of the toys and other objects in your home. Encourage this curiosity by providing safe objects to be mouthed.
- **Looks for the source of a sound:** The sounds in your home and outdoors have a bigger appeal. Your inquisitive baby will turn toward a sound and then actively look for the person or object that made the noise.
- **Studies small items:** From the buttons on your coats to the coins in your purse, small items may invite inspection. Note that your baby's fingers do not yet have the dexterity to grasp them, but his eyes are able to focus on them fairly well. Always keep these small objects, which are choking hazards, out of reach.
- **Gazes at objects in the distance:** Objects that were out of your baby's visual range warrant a longer look now. Noisy kitchen appliances, ceiling fans, and even the trees you pass by on a walk outside will entice your baby.
- **Is attracted to bright colors:** Bright colors continue to hold a great appeal for your baby's visual acuity. The ability to discern lighter shades of the same color is still a few weeks away.

Games and Activities

Textured Noms

Expose your baby to different textures that are safe to put in her mouth.

1. Gather some non-choking-hazard objects with different textures—metal, wood, cloth, and squishy—that your child can safely explore with her mouth.
2. Place these objects in a small basket in your baby's play area for tummy time, or offer them one at a time while in a supported seated position or while lying faceup.
3. Watch your baby's facial expressions as she explores these textures. Are any of the objects preferred?

Teeny Tiny Trinkets

Looking at tiny objects helps develop visual acuity.

1. While you are holding your baby, find a tiny object in your immediate vicinity. Examples include a leaf on a tree, a cabinet knob, or even the zipper pull on your coat. Brightly colored objects will be more appealing.
2. Name the object. For example, "This is a leaf."
3. If possible, move the object to attract his attention.
4. Watch for a reaction.

Note: Keep these small objects, which are choking hazards, out your baby's mouth.

Color Hunt

Bright colors are like nectar to your little bee.

1. Take a walk with your baby inside or out, taking time to slowly explore and find some brightly colored things.
2. Watch your baby's face while you explore. When her attention is drawn toward a brightly colored object, stop and admire it together.
3. Name the color of the object and offer your baby the chance to explore it physically in some way if possible. For example, "I see a red flower. Would you like to smell it?"

Language and Mental Development

All of those traditional baby games, such as Itsy Bitsy Spider, Pat-A-Cake, and belly tickling, will make a lot more sense now because your baby is developing a sense of humor. Some babies will be regularly smiling and responding but not quite giggling for a couple of months yet, so if laughter isn't a regular part of his expressions, there is no cause for concern.

You are likely to hear your baby make more vocalizations in response to your own voice, so continue the Parentese (see page 12) with exaggerated inflections, and take the opportunity when you can to ham it up. Explore the full range of your vocal ability by changing your pitch from low to high and back down again, or toot through a paper tube to shift the quality of your voice. Sing, whisper, squeal, chortle, and even growl if you like. He will appreciate all of these sounds and will try to imitate them.

Milestones

- **Imitates language sounds:** The ears and tongue continue to develop in sync, listening to human speech and then producing more varied sounds than before. Oral language development is highly individualized, but in general, the more sounds your baby listens to, the more motivated she is to imitate them.

- **Giggles with more predictability during simple games:** If you have a laughing baby, you will likely see a bit more consistency in the laughter. All babies learn to laugh and express joy, but yours may giggle more or less than others, and this is perfectly normal.

- **Becomes more aware of your inflection:** Your tone of voice tells your baby a lot about how you use language to communicate. For example, in English, a voice raises in pitch at the end of a sentence to indicate that the person is asking a question. Your baby can hear these subtleties, even if the meaning isn't quite clear yet.

- **Babbles to self:** Babbling, which may include any number of repetitive vocal sounds, is essential for language development. Even if no one is listening, your baby will be practicing putting together vowel sounds and experimenting with raising and lowering pitch.

- **Squeals loudly in delight:** Your baby will start to squeal to express herself—raising a vowel sound to a very high pitch and then lowering it again. She'll also be delighted and proud to hear herself make such a fun sound.

Games and Activities

Telephone

When you talk on the phone, you naturally exaggerate your inflection and tone, which is exactly what your baby likes to hear right now. Entertain him with an improvised conversation.

1. Introduce the game by saying, "What do you hear? Is it the phone ringing? Who could it be?" Pretend to pick up your phone and hold it to your ear.
2. Now pretend to have a conversation. Ad lib what your response would be to surprising or exciting news.
3. After about 30 seconds, hang up the pretend phone.

SURPRISING CHOKING HAZARDS

It's your child's job to put everything in reach in her mouth. Your challenge is to keep everything that's a potential choking hazard out of reach, and what's on that list might surprise you.

Potential choking hazards include objects smaller than 1.25 inches in diameter or 2.25 inches long. Solid objects that you can measure, such as coins, small balls, or toy parts (especially if you have an older child in the house) are fairly easy to recognize, but don't forget about little things like pet food, refrigerator magnets, pen caps, small batteries, and barrettes.

Choking hazards also include items made of materials that can become lodged in your baby's throat, including the filling of disposable diapers, paper, uninflated balloons, rubber bands, and hair bows.

To help keep play areas safe, regularly get down on the floor, or anywhere your baby is free to move around, and check for choking hazards from her perspective.

Babbling Back

Your baby naturally listens to you speak and tries to emulate what you say. Turn the tables.

1. Pick a time when your baby is in a playful mood and already vocalizing with coos, gurgles, squeals, or other sounds.
2. Sit nearby so that she can see your face and wait for her to "speak."
3. Imitate it as well as you can, and then stay quiet until you hear the next vocalization.
4. Many babies delight in this opportunity to have a babbling, back-and-forth conversation with a loved one. Play this game often if your baby enjoys it.

Mousie Ran Up

Elicit a squeal with this tickle game.

1. Using your index and middle fingers, walk your fingers on your own arm a bit to show your baby what you are going to do.
2. Now take one of her hands and hold it gently. As you say the rhyme, walk your fingers up her arm to the top of her head and then back down the other arm.
3. End the game with a gentle tickle on your baby's belly.

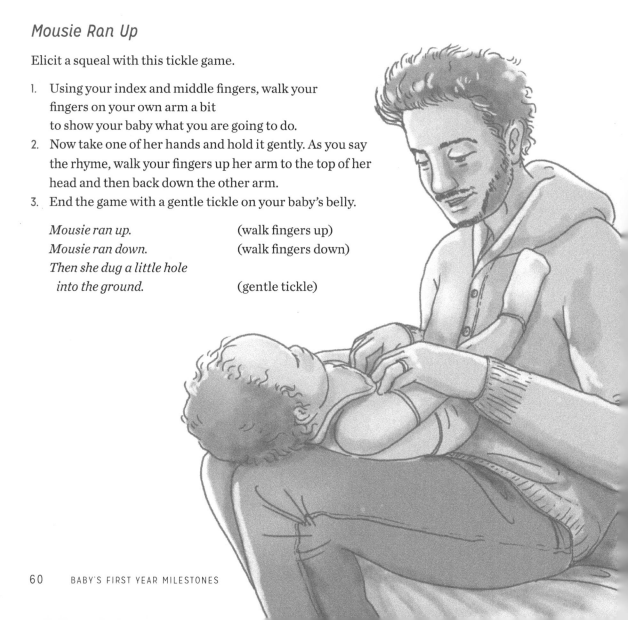

Mousie ran up.	(walk fingers up)
Mousie ran down.	(walk fingers down)
Then she dug a little hole	
into the ground.	(gentle tickle)

Social-Emotional Skills

By this time, you and your baby may feel like more of a team. Many parents feel that by this age, they are moving beyond the days when they felt helpless to pacify or understand their baby's needs. Your baby has a bit more patience during transitions and communicates with you much more clearly through both body language and vocalizations. She cries with more intention, not only to show unhappiness but also as a necessary tool to get you to engage and give her your full attention.

Taking your baby out into the world to greet and chat with other people, even passersby, is fairly easy. The separation anxiety that comes with a budding awareness of self is still a ways off yet. Right now, your baby is vocalizing and attempting to make eye contact with everyone.

Milestones

- **Communicates more clearly:** Expect your baby to make it more obvious what kind of attention he desires. You'll be aware immediately whether your baby is enjoying playing a game or is simply not impressed.
- **Fusses to get your attention:** Your baby fusses to get your attention as a tool until she learns other social skills.
- **Enjoys the company of unfamiliar people:** There will come a time when your baby is afraid of strangers and clings to you, but probably not this month. As you walk with your baby in public, you might find that he is attracting a lot of attention and thoroughly enjoys having "conversations" with others.
- **Recognizes parent's voice or touch:** You will always be home base, and your baby recognizes your presence by hearing your voice and feeling your touch. A hand placed on the back is recognized immediately as a source of comfort.
- **Eye contact intensity increases:** As your baby's receptive language skills ramp up, eye contact, among other forms of nonverbal communication, grows in intensity.

Games and Activities

Mirror Peekaboo

Peekaboo gets a makeover when you use different facial expressions in the mirror. Your baby is learning how to communicate and is aware of even small changes in your facial muscles. This is a great activity to add to your morning routine as you get ready to go to work.

1. Sit or stand in front of a large mirror where both of you can see your faces in the reflection.
2. Cover your face with one or two of your hands and play peekaboo, but this time change expressions every time you reveal your face. Try looking happy, sad, incredulous, depressed, confused, elated, unimpressed, and neutral.

Tip: This is an easy activity to do while using a baby carrier so that both of your hands are free.

GETTING THE GIGGLES

When your baby laughs, you are more likely to continue doing whatever it was you were doing that caused the chuckle. If crying is a signal that intervention is needed, laughter is your baby's way to ensure that the fun will continue.

Shared giggles are a bonding experience that can bring the two of you together emotionally. An expression of excitement, regular laughter makes parenting and growing up a more enjoyable experience. Encourage this healthy attitude toward life right from the very beginning.

Babies also have distinctly different temperaments, and laughter will help you get to know your own baby better. Some will find nearly everything you do hilarious, and others may need a warm-up period first. Not every game you play will elicit a giggle, but as you try out different ways of being silly, you will learn your baby's very own favorites.

Be a Bunny

This little bouncing game can be played anytime you are holding your baby.

1. Stand holding your baby in a place where you have room to move around without fear of tripping.
2. Chant the rhyme below while jumping up and down lightly on your feet.
3. When you get to the end, pause and look at your baby to see if she is enjoying this. If her body language communicates "Yes, again!" then repeat the rhyme.

Hop, hop, bunny hop.
And then we stop!
Again?

Two Little Eyes

This game entices your baby to maintain eye contact.

1. Lay your baby down faceup in front of you.
2. Talk to your baby about his eyes. For example, you might say, "I see your eyes. They are brown, just like your sister's. Eyes help us see the world around us. At night, we close them to go to sleep."
3. Now chant the following poem in an animated voice and perform the accompanying actions.

Two little eyes that blink, blink.	(blink your eyes)
Two little eyes that squint, squint.	(squint your eyes)
Two little eyes that open wide.	(open your eyes wide)
Two little eyes that go to sleep.	(close your eyes)
Night, night!	(pretend to go to sleep)

Notes

My baby is busy making these sounds:

_____

_____

_____

_____

_____

_____

_____

My baby smiles when I . . .

_____

_____

_____

_____

_____

_____

_____

_____

MONTH

5

Your Baby This Month

Babies turn on the charm. Those round bellies, beaming smiles, and twinkling eyes quickly win over exhausted parents and passing strangers alike. Your baby is simply bursting with personality, and the whole world is up for grabs. And grab he will. Everything your baby touches is likely to go right into that drooly mouth to be explored.

The mini pushups your baby has been doing during tummy time are paying off. Your roly-poly baby might be rolling over front to back and back to front, on purpose, to feel that spinning sensation or to reach a toy on the other side of the rug.

Your baby is also getting better at interpreting your moods. When you are happy, his smiling face reflects that joy back. When you feel anxious, he is likely more agitated and may even cry in distress. It's usually easier to interpret his moods as well because he is now better able to express himself through body language and vocalizations.

Challenges This Month

- **Mouthing everything:** More dexterity in the hands means that your baby is better at grabbing and pulling objects into the mouth. She instinctively gnaws on everything her fingers touch. Up your game by double-checking your babyproofing. Be especially vigilant about potential choking hazards (see page 59).
- **Freedom of movement:** Physical freedom in a safe, supervised environment is necessary for the natural development of gross motor skills. Try to use confined areas, such as play yards, sparingly. Your inquisitive baby needs room to roll, scoot, or crawl around.
- **Unnecessary equipment:** Avoid baby products that encourage you to put your baby in a confined space to practice a specific skill, such as a baby walker, jumper, exersaucer, or sitting positioner. There will be plenty of opportunities when your child has learned to walk to use fun equipment that allows her to explore unhindered, such as riding toys, pull and push toys, and walker wagons (see "Pushing to Walk" on page 179).

Highlights This Month

- **Music:** In earlier months, music was much more of a passive experience. Now your baby may kick or bounce along actively. She can tell the difference between classical music with an upbeat tune and more somber selections and will respond through body language and expression. But don't feel like you need to stick to the classical genre or variations on "Twinkle, Twinkle Little Star." Play any music that you find enjoyable and expose her to a variety of genres. She is aware and listening purposefully.
- **Interest in tasting:** Your baby has likely begun to express an interest in your food. You can nurture her curiosity by offering a clean spoon and cup to explore during your own mealtimes until you are ready to introduce solids.

Motor Skills

Your baby's mobility is increasing significantly. Full head control and stronger forearms mean that sitting without support is in the near future, if it is not happening already. To prepare for this, your baby might do stomach crunches and twist while on her back or perfect mini pushups during tummy time. Left on her own for enough practice time, she will eventually discover that she can push up, or roll and lift, into an unsupported seated position, but this does not usually happen until around seven to eleven months.

The timetable for this natural development is incredibly flexible and requires patience on your part. Some babies master this skill fairly quickly, and others take a long time to nail down the right technique. If your baby enjoys sitting up with you while you are playing together but does not have the strength to sit unassisted, she likely sits in the tripod position, with legs open and hands in between, pushing on the floor for extra support.

Both hands are still working in coordination to grasp objects, which makes sense for picking up and shaking larger objects, such as a textured ball. Many babies will work visibly hard to reach for and obtain a desired toy. You can encourage this natural desire by placing a few colorful objects just out of reach but within clear view. An uncluttered play space with just a few visible toys at one time helps your baby focus and choose a toy to go after with sudden, decisive ambition.

Milestones

- **Perfects mini pushups:** During tummy time, you likely see your baby straining to lift up higher using the muscles in the arms, neck, back, and abdomen.
- **Sits tripod style:** If your baby is not yet sitting unsupported, that is perfectly developmentally normal. Instead, you might see her leaning forward to balance with her hands in front in between her legs. Most babies are able to sit upright unassisted by nine months.
- **Rolls over more easily:** Most babies are rolling from front to back, and some are even rolling from back to front. Rolling over front to back often happens within moments, but rolling back to front may take her quite a bit of work. Note: Some babies skip rolling entirely.

- **Works hard to reach toys:** Dangling toys in front of your baby is still enticing, and she is likely to continue the batting practice. If she is sitting in your lap or freely moving about in a play area, you may notice quite a bit of hunting for interesting objects and intentional movements.
- **Grasps with two hands:** The ability to reach for and grasp an object with one hand will be coming for most babies next month. For now, you will likely see your baby reaching for objects and grasping them with a two-handed grip before shaking and releasing.

Games and Activities

Roll About

Sometimes the desire for a toy will motivate your baby to roll over. Why not give it a try and see?

1. Lie down with your baby on a soft surface where he has plenty of space to move around.
2. To encourage rolling, place a toy in front of him so that it captures his attention.
3. Slowly lift the toy into the air, up and over to the side, so that it remains slightly out of reach.
4. As your baby turns to follow the path of the toy, he may flip over.
5. Celebrate by giving him the toy to fully explore.

A Magic Trick

Repurpose an empty facial tissue box and a handful of scarves to provide a colorful surprise for those grasping fingers.

1. Knot a few scarves, or similar fabric pieces, together securely at the ends and place them inside a box with a hole on top, such as an empty tissue box. Leave a small piece of fabric poking out of the hole.
2. Offer this new "toy" for exploration, but hold the bottom of the box to make it easier to pull the bit of scarf peeking out.

3. Your baby may grab the scarf and begin pulling. If your baby does not know what to do, demonstrate how to reach for the scarf, grasp it with two hands, and pull upward, revealing more of the scarf.

4. If your baby is not interested or hasn't yet mastered reaching and grasping, try this activity another time. Either way, put away the box and scarf when you are done. Never leave your baby unattended with a tissue box, whether empty or full. The cardboard, the slit plastic that often covers the opening, and the tissues are all choking hazards, as is fabric.

Shake an Egg

Once your child can grasp with two hands and shake, shake, shake, an egg shaker may be just the percussion instrument you've been looking for.

1. Purchase or make an egg shaker for your baby. (A plastic Easter egg securely taped together with some pasta inside does the trick. Do not leave your baby unattended with the egg shaker, since dry pasta is a choking hazard.)

2. Give your baby the egg shaker to grasp, explore, and shake.

3. Optionally, put on some upbeat music and gently clasp your baby's hands as they hold the shaker to show him how to shake to a beat.

Sensory Development

From mouthing objects with more enthusiasm to tracking objects visually and locating sounds with more precision, your baby is on a roll. Even if she has been working on similar developmental accomplishments for a while, the process is now faster and more intuitive. Your baby is also discerning light and dark shades of colors, which makes art that uses shading or pastels much more interesting to look at.

Milestones

- **Benefits more from mouthing toys:** Your baby's sense of taste is being refined as he continues to put toys in his mouth to explore their range of textures and flavors. By practicing tongue and jaw movements, he's developing skills needed to eat solid food.

CHOOSING TOYS FOR YOUR BABY

When selecting toys for your baby to play with, look for objects that are fairly simple, open-ended, well-constructed, developmentally aligned, and purposeful. How much a toy costs has no relationship to how good of a match it is for your baby. Chances are that many of the objects you already own, especially an array of kitchen utensils and bowls, will be just perfect for your baby.

Babies learn when an action can be performed repeatedly with a natural consequence. For example, your baby might roll a simple rattle, bang it, shake it, drop it, or transfer it from one hand to the other. Each type of purposeful exploration will lead to a unique cause-and-effect learning experience.

When it comes to toys, quality definitely trumps quantity. Some commercially available toys targeted at babies are designed to teach higher-level language or numerical concepts that are more appropriate for the cognitive abilities of preschoolers. Others require batteries for operation, make noises, vibrate or sing songs, light up, and have multiple buttons to choose from. The packaging may even suggest that the toy itself will make your baby smarter. Be skeptical of these types of claims. A toy should encourage creative exploration, not tell a child how to play.

While simple toys are more developmentally appropriate, occasional use of highly stimulating items will not cause your baby any harm. Some families keep a few of their child's favorites and donate the rest. Others take out the batteries so that they no longer make noise or light up. Another popular option is to store them and bring them out for special times, such as during a long car ride. Every parent will have a slightly different perspective on and preference for the toys they enjoy using with their baby.

- **Tracks objects with more precision:** As distance vision has improved, you may notice your baby tracking objects from farther away. He works on this skill naturally when you are out and about, with so many things at varying distances vying for his attention.
- **Locates sounds more quickly:** Your baby is better than ever at searching for and locating the source of a sound. He is very easily distracted, though, so head turns and body shifts toward noises may feel lightning fast and catch you off balance.
- **Discerns subtler shades of color:** Bright colors continue to appeal to your baby, but by now the ability to see lighter and darker shades of one color is in full play.
- **Attracted to small items:** Not only are tiny objects easier to track visually, but they are also more appealing, and your baby wants to bring them right into her mouth. Continue to point out tiny objects, but keep them off-limits for hands-on exploring (see page 59).

Games and Activities

First Art Gallery

Present any art that you have in your home to your baby as her own personal gallery. She will especially enjoy the subtle variations in color.

1. Hold your baby when she's in a calm, alert state so that she can see the art.
2. Point at each picture and talk about what you see.

Note: Never hang artwork above a crib or changing table. Hang any artwork in the nursery with extra care. If a frame has a hanging wire, use an earthquake-safe picture hook for extra security.

Outside Observations

Inspect and track objects on an outdoor exploration.

1. Gather a blanket, a few toys, and a board book and head outside with your baby.
2. Lay the blanket under a tree. Read the book, play with the toys, and talk about the patterns created by the leaves above.
3. Look on the tree trunk and on the ground for any insects. Draw your baby's attention to them and watch them together.

Note: Remember your baby's sun protection before going outside.

Do You Hear What I Hear?

Who was that speaking? Locate these sounds together.

1. While a family member or friend is in another room talking, draw your baby's attention to the sound.
2. Ask your baby if he knows who is talking. Say, "Let's go find out who it is."
3. When you walk into the room, allow him to find the source of the sound, and then announce who it was. For example, "We heard Daddy talking to Grandma."

Language and Mental Development

Someday you will sit down and have a face-to-face conversation with your child, and today you are laying the groundwork. Your baby is likely spending much of the time listening to you speak, trying to imitate your voice, and repeating single sounds such as "ah" or "oh." She also finds a lot of funny things in the surrounding world and will not hesitate to burst into laughter or squeal in delight.

Learning how the world works is also a cognitive focus. Your curious baby is beginning to experiment with cause and effect. When a pot is hit with a wooden spoon, it makes a clanging sound. When a toy is swiped off of the kitchen counter, it hits the floor with a thud. When a ball is dropped, it bounces away. Actions and reactions may seem mundane to us as adults, but these simple experiences could not be more compelling to her right now.

Milestones

- **Laughs and squeals:** Your day-to-day life is likely punctuated by a variety of happy noises now. Your baby knows how to get your attention and the noises that make you respond most dramatically.
- **Repeats single sounds:** Your baby practices each new sound she learns to say with focused repetition. It may not matter to your baby whether you are there or not, as she will enjoy the babbling simply for the sake of perfecting those particular sounds.
- **Copies your voice:** Your baby is able to vocalize only the sounds that he has learned already, but make no mistake: He is actively listening to you speak and trying to mimic your voice. Keep talking and allowing time for "conversations" throughout the day.

- **Detects emotions with higher accuracy:** Distinguishing other people's emotions by their tone of voice becomes more important as your baby learns to interpret how humans use language to communicate feelings.
- **Becomes aware of cause and effect:** For the first few months of life, the senses were perceived quite separately, but your baby is beginning to connect the dots and enjoys playing games and exploring toys that have a clear cause and effect.

Games and Activities

Daily Book Basket

A love of books truly begins early in life. Model the importance of reading daily, including during playtime. You might also keep a basket of board books near your baby's sleeping area for a calming bedtime routine.

1. Put a handful of baby-friendly board books inside a basket where your baby typically plays.
2. Every day, reach inside the basket and select one to read out loud while he is having tummy time or sitting in your lap.
3. Read the book out loud and talk about what you see on each page. Go as slowly or as quickly as he seems to enjoy.

Note: Your baby is listening, even if his eyes are looking elsewhere. He also appreciates routine and repetition.

Slowly Goes the Turtle

This finger tickle game helps your baby hear fast and slow verbal paces.

1. Tell your baby "Here comes the turtle" to allow him to anticipate the game.
2. Take your index finger and middle finger and place them on your baby's left palm. Walk them up your baby's arm very slowly while you say the first line of this poem. Stop on his left shoulder.
3. Now put them in your baby's right palm. This time, run them up his right arm and over his head while you say the second line of the poem.

Slowly goes the turtle, up the hill.   (walk fingers up)
Quickly goes the little mouse, yes he will!   (walk fingers up)

Light On, Light Off

The concept of cause and effect is a big cognitive developmental leap forward. Use a light switch to demonstrate it.

1. Carry your baby over to a light switch on the wall. Allow her to touch it with her hands under your supervision.
2. Flip the switch to turn the light on. Point at the light.
3. Now flip the switch to "off" and give her a look of great surprise.
4. Repeat slowly. Flickering a light too fast can cause disorientation.

Social-Emotional Skills

Spending time with you, no matter what you are doing, is one of your baby's favorite things right now. Later, he will want to be more independent and go off exploring, but right now nothing is more reassuring or comforting than just hanging out next to you. When you leave the room, you may notice an expression of discontent on his face and perhaps even a bit of fussing, depending on the intensity of his emerging personality. He is just letting you know that your presence is expected and comforting.

Milestones

- **Requests playtime:** Your baby not only enjoys playtime now, she is also occasionally disappointed when it's over and it's time for another activity. She is able to tell you now through her animated body language when she would like to engage in or continue a game.
- **Expresses dislikes:** Up until now, discontent has primarily been expressed through crying or simply turning away. Your baby may be adding extra signals to her collection of techniques to show you her dislikes, such as making faces or vocalizing.
- **Anticipates and relies on regular routines:** Babies like routines. The structure gives them a sense of security. A new awareness and reliance on these consistencies is evident. It may not be obvious while you're at home, but you will certainly be able to tell if there is an unexpected disruption.
- **Acts more attached to family members:** It's still a bit early for real separation anxiety, but you may notice that your baby is more insistent about being wherever you are and may find that she wants you to carry her more often.

- **Reveals unique personality traits:** Is your baby a little shy? Overly sensitive to stimulation? Super social? You will have deeper glimpses into the personality of this little person you are raising, and it may be a surprise to recognize similarities to or differences from your own characteristics.

Games and Activities

The Good Morning Game

Your baby is becoming more aware of routines. This game signals that it's time for your morning to begin.

1. Say good morning to your baby first. Stretch out the moments of that first greeting of the day.
2. Your baby might want to be changed and fed first, so if that is your habit, start there. When you are ready to play the game, pick her up and carry her around the house.
3. Notice what her eyes alight on, no matter what it is, and say good morning to it. For example, if she looks at the cabinet, say, "Good morning, cabinet. Let's see what's inside."

QUIET TIME

Your baby's ability to play has taken a significant jump, but keep in mind it's important not to overstimulate her. She doesn't want or need be entertained all the time. In fact, healthy development comes from balancing a mix of interactive and quiet experiences.

Without a clear concept of past, present, and future, your baby is literally living moment by moment. Periods of excitement and energy will naturally be followed by periods of quiet awareness.

During one of these quiet moments each day, take a bit of time to just sit and be with your baby without feeling the need to talk. Watch where your baby's gaze shifts and for how long. Notice the tiny muscle movements. Appreciate the quiet space and good company. Breathe.

Evening Song

Routines are meaningful to your baby. Singing the same song or playing the same music each night can help cue him that it's time to wind down for bed.

1. Hold your baby and sway back and forth.
2. Tell him that the day is ending and the sun is going around to the other side of Earth, darkening our sky so that we can sleep.
3. Sing this little song to your own improvised tune.

> *Good night, good night, good night to you*
> *The sun goes down and we will, too*
> *We read and we played*
> *We danced and we swayed*
> *And the day says good night to you*

Ride a Little Horsey

The premise of this traditional baby game is anticipation, and to play it, your baby must have full head control and be able to sit up in a supported position.

1. Sit down on the floor with your legs out in front of you. Place your baby on your lap and fully support her back and hips with your hands.
2. Ask if she would like to have a horsey ride. If she looks at you happily and wiggles excitedly, she is probably in the right mood for the game.
3. Chant the Ride a Little Horsey rhyme while you bounce your knees lightly up and down. Say the words "fall dooooooown" slowly, with inflection. Then lean over with her slightly toward one side or toward your knees. Never let go of your baby and let her fall for real. The movements are very slight and all in good fun.
4. Before repeating the game, ask your baby if she would like to do it again. Observe her body language and perhaps vocalizations to see if she'd like to continue.

Ride a little horsey into town
Better watch out, you might fall down!
(variation on a traditional rhyme)

SAYING BYE-BYE

If you need to go somewhere, whether briefly or before you leave for a workday, it's important not to sneak out. Always tell your baby that you are going and when you will be back. Creating your own special good-bye routine will also ease the transition.

Say the same thing ("See you later, alligator") and do the same actions (rub noses, kiss each cheek, one big hug) each time you go, and then leave with confidence. In time, your baby will come to understand that ritual means you are leaving but that she can trust you to come back, which will be immensely reassuring. But don't be surprised if your baby wishes to have a longer snuggle when you return.

Notes

My baby is amused when I . . .

_____

_____

_____

_____

_____

_____

_____

Some of my baby's personality traits seem to be . . .

_____

_____

_____

_____

_____

_____

_____

_____

MONTH

6

Your Baby This Month

When you're about half a year in, the anxieties that came with the previous six months may begin to fade. Your squishy, squirmy baby is not as fragile. Enjoy your baby's relative portability while getting out and about. It will still take time to pack a diaper bag and get her fed and dressed, and yet visiting friends or exploring the neighborhood together will probably feel a lot less stressful. She may be more easily entertained, absorbing all of the sensory experiences offered within a simple outing.

Challenges This Month

- **Drooling:** Where there is teething, there is drool. Sometimes near-constant drool. Sometimes so much drool that the tops of shirts or bibs are soaked every hour. Keep extra on hand for quick changes.
- **Biting:** Your baby has been learning jaw movements in preparation for solid food. One of those skills: biting. If your baby bites you, for example, while he's nursing, respond in a consistent way to discourage the behavior, but don't make too big of a deal out of it, or you risk reinforcing it. Hold him away from you (remove him from the situation) and tell him biting people is not allowed. Give him a teething toy or return to nursing. If he bites again, calmly repeat.
- **Mood swings:** If it seems like one moment your baby is happy and the next she is crying, only to be happy again a minute later, you might be reeling from her mood swings. Expect your baby to have big but short-lived emotional states. It should be fairly easy to redirect attention or calm the current mood with a good cuddle.

Highlights This Month

- **Bigger bathtub:** If you've been bathing your baby in a baby-size tub and he sits up without support, consider making the transition into an adult-size bathtub. You might get in there, too, especially the first time, to provide reassurance with your presence. Or place the little tub into the big tub to allow your baby to adjust to the new surroundings. Either way, your baby is bound to react to the sensation of being in a larger amount of water. Many babies love it. If yours doesn't, be patient, keep bath times short and offer comfort. Never leave your baby unattended near water.
- **Bouncy playtime:** With solid head control, your little one will feel so much more secure in your arms. Go ahead and indulge in some bouncy games with baby on your knee, or take her on an "airplane" ride around the room. Remember to keep it fairly gentle. Rough-and-tumble play will need to wait until your baby's muscles are much stronger.

Motor Skills

The coordinated movements your baby is able to engage in are a great boon to playtime. Of course, your baby is likely still experiencing some amount of frustration at her inability to reach certain items, and this will continue well through toddlerhood. However, the increased ability to pick up and manipulate toys without your direct assistance is a big step. It's still on the early side for most babies, but soon you may even see her transferring an object from one hand to the other.

The ability to sit up gives your baby a new vantage point. If she is still too wobbly to enjoy a seated position other than in your lap, you don't need to prop her up or work on this specifically. The time your baby is spending doing other things such as kicking, rolling, scooting, reaching, or lifting strengthens those back and abdominal muscles. It will be worth the wait when you see her master this skill and feel the empowerment that comes with self-discovery. Remember that whatever physical activity your baby is most interested in doing is the activity that is just perfect for that day's agenda.

Milestones

- **Rolls both ways:** Your roly-poly baby might be rolling from front to back and back to front quite often. Some babies use rolling as a method of locomotion to reach the toys they want, and others just enjoy the sensation.
- **Sits with less support:** If your baby has been sitting tripod style (legs open and hands in between, pushing on the floor for extra support), you might notice more stability. Toppling over becomes less and less likely as muscle strength develops.
- **Rakes small objects toward self:** Your baby's fingers might act somewhat like a yard rake. Like scattered leaves on the ground, small objects can be scraped into the palm for closer inspection.
- **Coordinates upper-body movements:** As the muscles in your baby's arms, wrists, palms, and fingers get stronger and more refined, they work together to allow him to grasp objects with more intention and bring them up to the mouth for continued exploration.
- **Transfers objects:** While most babies continue to grasp objects with both hands, some babies begin transferring them from one hand to the other. This requires the ability to clutch with one hand and release it into the coordinated clutch of another hand—an admirable and extremely useful skill.

Games and Activities

Toy Chase

This upper body-strengthening activity could mesmerize your baby with the simple magic of flotation.

1. Place a low cooking sheet, pan, or tray with a raised edge on top of a bath towel laid on the floor. Fill it with about one-half to one inch of water.
2. Add a few small toys that float. Make sure that they are large enough not to be choking hazards.
3. Place your baby tummy down in front of the tray.
4. Show him how to push the floating toys around and ask him if he would like to give it a try.

Note: Never leave your baby unattended with water.

Muffin Stuff

An empty muffin tin offers all sorts of play possibilities while your baby concentrates on transferring objects from one space into another.

1. Put a regular-size muffin tin on the floor.
2. Place soft, squishy toys inside a few of the cups in the muffin tin. You do not need to fill all of the holes. Just a few will do.
3. Sit with your baby in front of the tin. Tell him you would like to show him something. Demonstrate how to pick up the toy and replace it inside the cup.
4. Allow him to investigate the toys inside the tin.

Roll Away Bottle

This is a game you can truly take anywhere to encourage your baby's gross motor skills—especially on a picnic on a warm day in the shade.

1. Fill a reusable water bottle halfway with cool or tepid water. Tighten the lid securely.
2. Place the bottle horizontally in front of your baby while he is on his belly.
3. Demonstrate how the bottle can roll by pushing on it slightly.
4. Allow your baby time to explore the bottle with all of his senses. When he is ready to change activities, empty the water, cap the lid securely, and stow away the bottle.

READING TIPS

Is your baby more interested in mouthing books than in reading them right now? This is perfectly normal behavior. When displaying books, you may want to make sure you have durable board books available for self-exploration and keep the thinner-paper books up high for you to retrieve yourself.

Books can foster stimulating conversations about a variety of topics. Since it will be quite some time before your baby will be able to read words himself, it does not matter if you are reading the words on the page exactly as they are written.

One technique you might try is to describe the pictures as you turn the pages and draw connections to real life. For example, if you see a picture of a sheep, you might say, "I see a sheep. Sheep are woolly. Sheep say 'baa, baa.' In the spring, the wooly sheep are shorn, and that wool is spun into yarn. You can knit the yarn into a scarf or a sweater. I have a scarf made out of the wool from a sheep. Would you like to feel it?"

And while we're on the subject of textures, definitely invest in a touch-and-feel type board book. It turns the reading experience into a sensory experience.

You might find that a young baby does not want you to read the book in order, instead pawing at the book to skip ahead. Skipping around is perfectly fine. In fact, feel free to pass over the board book in favor of narrating a news article or novel. Any read-aloud will reveal your inflection, cadence, rhythm, and vocabulary.

Don't expect the reading experience to be one of sustained focus, either. You can keep reading even as your child crawls away to play with another toy, and because those little ears are so sensitive to sound, all the benefits still apply.

Finally, expect that sometime in the last half of this year, about the same time that your baby is learning to recognize and respond to words, you may find yourself reading the same book over and over. Short, predictable rhyming books are wonderful for babies at this stage.

Sensory Development

Traditional baby-friendly bouncing songs, clapping chants, and anticipation games have been passed from generation to generation. Parents and babies continue to enjoy this subtly structured playtime. Now neuroscience research confirms our instincts: By engaging several senses at one time for brief, focused periods, we are helping different parts of the brain connect. For example, when you bounce your baby on your lap in rhythm, sing a song, and end with an anticipated new sensation, your baby is experiencing visual, auditory, and tactile stimulation.

By the end of six months, your baby has also become more attuned to the differences between types of fabric, including cotton, satin, wool, corduroy, and leather. Allowing him to sit and feel grass, sand, or other outdoor surfaces will help him develop his texture discrimination abilities.

Those little fingers are also exploring all of the nooks and crannies of every personal body part. The backs of the ears, inside the belly button, and even the genitals will be fully explored. This interest is important and normal. By allowing some diaper-free time for self-touching, you are helping your baby establish a healthy self-image right from the beginning.

Milestones

- **Explores own body:** It's not just the toes anymore. Your baby is becoming aware of body movement, body function, and skin sensations, evidenced by repeated small movements and seeking fingers exploring the physical self.
- **Tracks a falling object farther:** Depth perception continues to increase. Your baby likely visually follows a toy that is dropped from higher places, closely watching the quick descent to the floor.
- **Feels textures with more attention:** Texture exploration, including the shape and size of objects, may begin to fascinate your baby. Offering a variety of textures for sensory play for her to mouth and touch using different body parts is often satisfying.
- **Reacts differently to different voices:** By now some babies are reacting differently to different types of voices. For example, you may notice your baby distinguishing between male and female or younger and older voices.
- **Enjoys rhythmic movement:** The ability to clap hands at a steady tempo is still quite a ways off yet. In order to develop this musical skill, your baby needs you to offer physical ways to feel a steady beat, both fast and slow. When singing or listening to songs, she is likely to especially enjoy being bounced or rocked to the beat.

Games and Activities

Your Body

Your baby may have a particular fascination with body parts. This game introduces relevant vocabulary.

1. Look into your baby's eyes to solicit attention. While your baby is sitting or lying down, tell your baby you are going to touch his body.
2. Place your hands at the top of his head and lightly run them down his whole body, from head to toe. Say, "This is your body."
3. Now place your hands on different body parts and name them. For example, say "This is your arm" while gently rubbing his arm.

Note: Your baby may not yet understand the connection between your actions and your words and the sensations that he feels, but the vocabulary and interaction will be meaningful regardless.

Carousel Ride

This bouncy game helps your baby develop a sense of rhythm and affirms that it is your baby's choice to participate.

1. Sit down on the floor with your legs straight out in front of you.
2. Now place your baby on your lap just in front of your knees. If he is sitting well without support, hold his hands in yours just to make sure he doesn't topple over during the game.
3. Ask your baby if he'd like to go on a carousel ride. Observe him to see if he's in the mood to play.
4. Chant the Carousel Ride poem, and at the same time bounce your knees up and down in a quick, steady rhythm.
5. When you get to the words "or maybe not . . ." slow down the tempo considerably. Say, "Are you ready to do it again?" and wait until your baby cues you he's ready to begin again.

Round and round the carousel
Baby's on a horse
Will he go around again?
Yes, of course!
Or maybe not . . .

The Beat Is in the Feet

Classical, hip-hop, indie, jazz, blues—music from any genre will do as long as it has a strong rhythm.

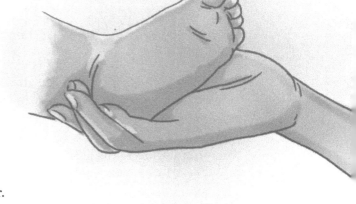

1. Lay your baby down on her back.
2. Hold one of your baby's feet up in the air with one hand. With the other, lightly tap the bottom of her foot in time with the rhythm.
3. After a minute or so, switch feet. To vary this activity, pick up both feet and tap them together.

Here are a few musical suggestions from the classical genre:

Eine kleine Nachtmusik, Movement 1 by Mozart
"Ride of the Valkyries" by Wagner
"The Washington Post" by Sousa

Language and Mental Development

Humans have long wondered why we don't retain memories of our babyhood. No one can answer this exactly, but we know that during the middle of the first year, babies can begin to remember simple sensations associated with self-caused actions. For example, "When I bring a piece of this mushy substance to my mouth, the taste is mild and sweet." From this point on, your baby may purposefully bat at a bell to hear the jingle again or reach for a favorite toy to reexperience the texture in his mouth.

The budding awareness of self is still merely emerging. Up until now, your baby has more or less felt literally connected to you. Even the massages and gentle tickles have not been associated with your movements directly. The first awareness of self begins with the exploration of one's own body, which coincides with budding communication and language skills.

You may begin to hear utterances from your baby's vocal cords that sound more and more like speech. It's still too early for these words to have associated meanings, as excited as you are to hear them. Even so, this is the beginning of his journey to identify as an individual person. So keep playing simple games and talking about everyday experiences. He will thoroughly enjoy the personal interaction, the opportunity for giggles, and the repetition of feel-good experiences.

Milestones

- **Looks briefly for a dropped toy:** The increased depth perception your baby has acquired aids him when looking for a toy that has been dropped. There is a new awareness that objects that disappear go somewhere, although the concept of exactly where they go has not fully developed.
- **Enjoys simple games:** Playing with your baby does not need to be complicated to hold his interest. In fact, the more predictable and simple the game, the better.
- **Differentiates between self and others:** Up until this point, it has not even occurred to your baby that your body is a separate entity from his. Now the sense of self begins to develop. Physical sensations have more meaning and are remembered along with the self-initiated activity that caused them.
- **Giggles more often:** Once the giggles start, they are often hard to stop.
- **Repeats single sounds more frequently:** If your baby is not babbling yet, there is still no cause for concern, but single syllable sounds like "mah" and "dah" are common for about half of babies this age.

Games and Activities

Here Is Yours, Here Is Mine

Your baby is just becoming aware that you are an entirely separate person from himself. This turn-taking game emphasizes the differences between the two of you. It would also be an easy activity to do while buckling your baby into his car seat.

1. While your baby is in an inquisitive, focused mood, gaze right into his eyes to get his attention.
2. Now touch his cheek and say, "Here is your cheek."
3. Next, touch your own cheek and say, "Here is my cheek."
4. Play this game with different body parts, including hair, eyes, nose, mouth, ears, neck, etc. Allow your baby to mimic your movements if desired.

Down It Goes

Let's put that increased visual depth perception to good use by looking for a disappearing object.

1. During playtime, drop a scarf or playsilk from adult height.
2. Watch it float slowly down to the ground. Your baby may track the movement.
3. Try this activity again with your baby in your arms. This time tell your baby what will happen first. Then, intentionally drop a jingle bell or rattle that makes a soft sound. Watch your baby look briefly for the dropped toy, then retrieve it together.

Three Useful Things

A basket of objects can be intriguing and offer opportunities for receptive language skills.

1. Place three objects you use with your baby in a basket.
2. Take them out of the basket and name them one by one. For example, "This is a cup. This is a spoon. This is a brush."
3. Now role play what you do with each one. For example, "Where is the cup? What do we do with the cup? Drink. Where is the spoon? What do we do with the spoon? Eat."
4. Put the objects back inside the basket and allow your baby to choose an object to explore.

Social-Emotional Skills

The development of empathy for the emotional states of others takes time, but you can see it emerging already. Your baby has spent the last several months watching your face and evaluating your emotional states. Now, along with the awareness of self as a separate individual, she is aware of and emulating and reflecting your moods. When you cry or look dejected, your baby authentically experiences distress and mimics your frowns. When you are excited and full of energy, this is contagious for her as well. The two of you are emotionally in sync, and this is an important milestone in social-emotional development.

Simple games that involve taking turns begin encompassing more of your time because babies simply love them. Your little one is likely to be more demanding of your time now than before, wanting to hang out with you where your face is easily visible rather than sitting and looking around at the world.

Milestones

- **Mimics and shares your emotions:** When you're feeling blue, your baby's face may emulate the same expression of sadness. You may even hear some empathetic cries. The reverse is true as well. When joy is on your face, he may giggle and coo in response.
- **Engages in a turn-taking game:** The games you play with your baby now as you make noises back and forth and mimic each other's actions lay the groundwork for real conversations.
- **Studies your reactions to others:** You may notice the intensity of your baby's gaze on you increasing once again, just as it did in those newborn months, as you move through your day. This time, however, he has a new awareness of the world. He is learning how you handle personal stressors and how you engage with others.
- **Craves stimulation:** Is it beginning to feel like your baby wants all of your attention all of the time? You may notice some jealousy creeping in when you give your attention to another person or a task. Your baby no longer sits happily while the world moves by. There is a definite desire to be right in the thick of it.
- **Lets you know when a game is over:** When your baby is done with an activity and ready to move on to something else, you see a more decisive movement away from the source of stimulation. Even when she seems a bit grouchy, this is such a useful development because you more easily know how much playtime is too much.

Games and Activities

Hey, What's on Your Head?

Give your baby your undivided attention while you take turns getting silly with a scarf.

1. While your baby is watching you, put a scarf on top of your head.
2. Bend down low and allow her to grab it and pull it off. If she does not, pull it off yourself.
3. Say, "Here I am!"
4. Now it's your baby's turn. Put the scarf on her head and let her pull it off.

What's Inside?

This turn-taking game will stimulate your baby's sense of hearing.

1. Take two medium-size containers and put in a few objects that make a rattling sound when shaken. One should sound loud and clunky and the other soft and hissing. Try macaroni, rice, dried beans, or rocks. Never leave your baby unattended with these items, and put them away when you're done with the activity.
2. Sit facing your baby on the floor in front of one of the containers. Without shaking it, offer it to him for exploration. If he shakes it and hears the noise, smile widely and with eyebrows raised.
3. Now do the same with the second container. Observe his reactions. Is he more curious about the noise or the movement?

Breathe and Soothe

Is your baby turning away from visuals or sounds? Try this soothing back massage.

1. Take your baby to a quiet room and lay yourself down. Place her on top of you so that you are belly to belly.
2. Take a deep abdominal breath and let it out slowly. She will feel your chest cavity rising and falling.
3. Rub her back in coordination with every breath you take. Up as you breathe in, down as you breathe out.

Notes

Textures my baby has enjoyed feeling this month include . . .

A game my baby wanted to play this month was . . .

MONTH

7

Your Baby This Month

Easy grins, infectious giggles, and an awareness of the world just out of reach characterize babies in the seventh month. You may find yourself looking at the world differently as you evaluate the potential interest of everything—vibrant flowers, the sounds your car makes, textures of foods—for your curious baby.

Be prepared for the time when your baby is or will soon be mobile enough to reach for objects that are unsafe or off-limits. Create safe "yes" spaces that encourage free exploration. It won't be long before your baby is climbing up the furniture, but most babies this age are more interested in the ability to sit up straight unsupported and to work on crawling and hand-strength skills. Even so, there will be activities that cannot be allowed, such as hair pulling or biting. Provide something that fulfills the need to pull or bite, like a scarf for tug-of-war or a teething toy.

Challenges This Month

- **Requires more supervision:** Your baby's newfound mobility means his caregivers need to be even more vigilant than before. Revisit babyproofing every room of your house. Check for floor-level hazards, including stairway entrances, unsecured furniture, window-covering cords, electrical cords, and choking hazards (see page 59). Also secure household chemicals and cleaners, taking particular care with soap pods for the dishwasher or laundry.
- **First foods:** Solid foods may now be on the menu. Talk to your baby's doctor about the right time for your baby to start solids.
- **Distrustful of strangers:** Expect your baby to be a little clingier. When in social situations with people who aren't too familiar, allow plenty of time for him to get to know a new person from the safety of your arms.

Highlights This Month

- **Easily entertained:** Nearly anything can become a toy. From the crunchy leaves outside to the stackable cups in your kitchen, as long as the object is safe to mouth, you will find your baby easily engaged.
- **Sitting up:** Stronger back and abdominal muscles make sitting up for longer periods easier. Your baby will enjoy bouncing on your knees, and a bit of hand-holding may be enough support to keep your little one upright.
- **Listens to stories:** It is still a bit early to expect sustained, focused attention, but make no mistake—your baby is actively listening. Keep modeling an interest in books, pointing at pictures, and reading out loud. Pretty soon you will find your baby initiating this activity. Developing a lifelong love of reading can really be this simple.

Motor Skills

Plopping your baby down for a few minutes may feel much easier once he is truly sitting up unsupported. Almost all babies sit up alone for a few minutes by the end of the ninth month, so if your baby is not quite there at this point, he is still well within the normal range. Crawling is also in the near future, although it's still a bit too early for most babies to master it. Once these gross motor skill leaps have been made, there's generally no going back. Most babies absolutely love being upright and perfect the crawling position with intense focus.

Fine motor skills are also taking a leap. Your busy bee is manipulating toys with more dexterity and purpose than ever before. Most babies grasp with the whole hand, transferring objects from hand to hand as they play. But some babies noticeably start to use a more subtle, defter grasp by the end of this month, starting with raking small objects closer and then attempting to pick them up with more direct finger-and-thumb action.

Milestones

- **Sits unsupported:** By now many babies are sitting up on their own without any additional support for several minutes. You might notice yours looking more relaxed in this position, happily scanning his surroundings. Most will have learned this skill by the time they are eight months old.
- **Assumes the crawling position:** Your baby may or may not already have been scooting or spinning using those strong arm muscles, but you might notice his back legs taking a more active role in this process. While in a crawling position, many babies this age can now reach out to grab a toy.
- **May show first signs of future pincer grasp:** Correct and effective use of the thumb and index finger is still elusive. Most babies still use the palmar grasp (whole hand clutching) and raking motions to pick up objects. By the end of this month, you may see your child's concentrated efforts to open and close the thumb and four fingers in a clawlike motion, but it is too early to expect it. The development of the pincer grasp is often a lengthy process that is mastered by the end of the first year.
- **Easily transfers objects:** The ability to transfer an object from one hand to another has big payoffs during playtime. Now when your baby grasps a toy with one hand, it can be transferred to the other hand for continued exploration. This ability is immensely satisfying for her, as the impulse to reach for and obtain objects, bring them to the mouth, and bang them together is very strong.

Games and Activities

Down Goes the Tower

Help your baby practice some demolition skills from a seated position.

1. Sit on the floor next to your baby. Stack four to five rubbery or wooden cube-shaped blocks one on top of the other.
2. Demonstrate how the tower can be knocked down.
3. Stack the blocks up again and this time wait to see if she will knock them down by pushing them over with a hand or foot.

Kitchen Treasure Basket

While you are busy in the kitchen, provide entertainment with safe kitchen items.

1. Place three baby-safe kitchen tools—for example, a wooden spoon, a spatula, and a slotted spoon—inside a basket.
2. Sit down next to your baby on the kitchen floor on top of a blanket.
3. Explore the kitchen tools together. Name them, feel them, and put them back inside the basket.
4. Resume your kitchen duties and let him explore these items alone.
5. Keep this basket of objects in the kitchen for ready-made entertainment while you cook. Every so often, rotate in new objects.

Roll the Ball

If your baby can sit up unsupported, now is a great time to practice rolling a ball back and forth. You will want to use a soft or rubbery ball that is easy to grasp with two hands.

1. Sit down on the floor facing your baby.
2. Hold up the ball so that her attention is focused upon it.
3. Now take turns rolling this ball back and forth from just a few feet away from her.
4. As you roll the ball, sing the song below. Feel free to make up your own melody, or sing it to the tune of "Do You Know the Muffin Man."

   Do we know how to roll a ball,
   Roll a ball, roll a ball?
   Do we know how to roll a ball?
   Roll a little ball.

Yes, we know how to roll a ball,
Roll a ball, roll a ball.
Yes, we know how to roll a ball.
Yes, we do indeed!

Sensory Development

The sensations of the world continue to delight your baby. Visually tracking a toy when you move it either horizontally or vertically is a much quicker process than ever before, as depth perception continues to improve. This skill comes in at just the right time because your baby may become more familiar with guiding a cup or spoon into the mouth, an activity much aided by adept visual tracking.

You may notice her engaging in multisensory self-stimulation by manipulating toys with both the hand and the mouth, often at the same time. You may notice that she makes no distinction between an edible item and a nonedible item. To your baby, all the flavors and textures of the world are for hand-to-mouth exploration.

Isolated sensory experiences are also extremely beneficial. To help her develop the focus needed to track rapidly moving objects and pinpoint sounds coming from unseen places, you might make a habit of pausing now and then when out and about. Slow down enough, for example, to observe a car passing swiftly by. When you hear a bird chirp up above, take some time to hunt for it in the trees.

Milestones

- **Tracks rapid movements:** Your baby's eyes are becoming adept at noticing and accurately following even fast movements from one side to another.
- **Distracted less often:** Previously, any little noise might distract your baby from the task at hand. She is less tempted to turn away from the sound she is focused on. This comes in handy while you are talking to and playing with your baby in a room where other people are talking.
- **Looks for the source of hidden sounds:** Your baby is responding to a variety of sounds, including vocal variations in pitch, volume, and tone, and is recognizing familiar sounds made by objects. When these sounds are heard, she will now be actively looking for the source of the noise even when it is outside of visual range.

- **Examines objects with hand and mouth:** The way your baby is learning about objects is changing along with the new motor skills. The hands, working more in coordination with each other, will bring a toy up to be tasted and back down to be twisted, turned, banged, transferred, and brought back up to the mouth. This multi-sensory engagement is fun for her.
- **Practices self-feeding:** If you have introduced solid foods, you may see an interest in picking up food or guiding a spoon toward the mouth. Drinking out of a cup may also be intriguing.

Games and Activities

Explore Floating

Placing an object in water allows for a very different sensory experience. Many babies find this water trick funny.

1. Fill your kitchen sink (or a large container) with lukewarm water.
2. Place one palm-size floating object on the surface of the water.
3. Carry your baby over to the sink or container so that he can see the object.
4. Push the toy down to the bottom and watch it pop back up. After demonstrating this a few times, allow your baby to reach over and grab the toy to explore with both hands and mouth. When you're done empty the sink of water. Never leave your baby unattended near water.

Food Playground

If your baby has been introduced to solid foods, encourage him to practice self-feeding.

1. Select two foods that have already been introduced to your baby that have considerably different textures and tastes. For example, mashed sweet potato and mashed avocado.
2. Place a dollop of one type of food on one side of a tray and a dollop of another type of food on the other side.
3. Allow your baby to use her fingers to touch the different textures, play with them on the tray, and bring them up to her mouth for self-feeding.
4. Observe your baby's reactions to gauge her preferences.

A Tiny Cup

Your baby is interested in watching you drink, but don't go for the sippy cup just yet. Let her experiment with a real cup.

1. Fill a very tiny, thick-walled cup (shot glass size) with about one inch of water.
2. For the first introduction, sit comfortably with your baby near the floor with a soft surface underneath, such as a blanket or towel.
3. Hold the cup in front of her at chest level. Allow her to grasp the cup with two hands and guide it to her mouth.

Note: Your baby may be more interested in dumping out the water than drinking it, and that is just fine. Always empty out the water when you're done.

Language and Mental Development

Words are beginning to have a greater significance. The words that you have been speaking to your baby since birth begin to take on clearer meanings, although the overall intent may still be a bit fuzzy. Babies develop receptive (listening) language skills far before expressive (talking) ones, so if you get the feeling that she somehow knows a lot more than she lets on, your hunch is correct.

Your baby's expressive language skills are moving right along as well. It simply takes time and practice for the ear, mouth, and throat to work in sync and learn how to produce the sounds that are used in language. Remember that your baby is still able to hear all of the sounds in the environment. It is a slow process of pruning out the ones that are irrelevant, and it takes even longer to reproduce them. The chunks of sounds we call words most likely cannot be duplicated yet, but you may start to hear her combining sounds together that sound like real words.

Milestones

- **Responds to own name:** If you say your baby's name, you may notice an extra alert expression or more focused eye contact. The association between this special word and the awareness of self is already starting to develop.
- **Becomes aware of the word "no":** Don't expect obedience in any form from your child, but the meaning of this special limit-setting word will become clear in the next few months. By limiting your own use of this word to dangerous or unsafe activities, you are actually attaching greater importance to it. Make sure to follow through by physically removing your child from the unsafe area or the object from view.
- **Babbles chains of consonants:** The ability to repeat sounds quickly and change from one to another transforms your baby's vocalizations into something that sounds a lot more like talking. It is around this age that many parents are delighted to hear the socially significant sounds "mamama" or "dadada" emerge. The meaning of these special words may not quite be there yet, but it is soon to come as you encourage the repeated use enthusiastically.

- **Imitates patterns of speech:** Conversations involve a lot more than just words. You may hear your baby vocalizing and pausing at the end of a string of sounds to raise or lower pitch, as though making a statement or asking a question.
- **Finds partially hidden objects:** Babies are beginning to understand that objects can be hidden and revealed. If you place a toy halfway underneath a blanket, your baby may move toward it, uncover the other half, and be excited to do it all over again.

Games and Activities

Five Little Acorns

Fingerplays are fun and help develop your baby's memory and vocabulary. Tell this finger story about what happens to five little acorns.

1. Sit with your baby in front of you so that you can maintain eye contact throughout this game.
2. Hold his hand, palm up, gently in one of your hands. With your other hand, start the game by placing your fingertips inside his palm.
3. Now use your index finger and thumb to wiggle each of his fingers in turn while you chant the rhyme.
4. End on the word "none" by lightly clapping your palm against his palm.

   Five little acorns in baby's hand
   One for the squirrel to run and hide
   One for the woodpecker to peck inside
   One for the deer to nibble and run
   One for mousie to eat in the sun
   And one for my baby and now there are none

I'll Whisper Your Name

Your baby is becoming more attuned to listening to her own name.

1. While your baby is playing on the floor, walk across to the other side of the room, even hide behind a curtain or furniture.
2. Say your baby's name very quietly—in the barest whisper. Check to see if her attention is drawn toward you. If it isn't, raise the volume of your voice, but keep things quiet.
3. When she looks up at you, say, "I see [your baby's name]!"

Hidden Objects

What's in there? Your baby will want to peek and discover.

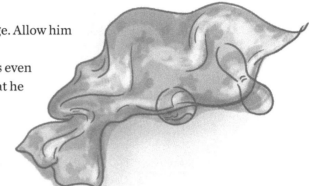

1. Sit or lie with your baby on the floor.
2. Select one of the toys within his visual range. Allow him to touch and perhaps taste the toy.
3. Now cover the toy with a very thin, perhaps even sheer scarf or piece of fabric. Make sure that he can see the shape of the toy underneath.
4. Say, "I see something under the scarf. I wonder what it could be."
5. As your baby explores the scarf and hidden toy, wait until the object is uncovered before announcing the name of the toy.

Social-Emotional Skills

During the first few months of life, a baby's expressions and vocalizations, especially those of distress, conveyed an intense need for immediate adult attention. Crying was an automatic response, usually reserved for physical discomfort or a desire for security. Now new desires have emerged, along with a new awareness of the surrounding world. Your baby has wants, not just needs, and the two are becoming distinct from each other, along with the ability to express emotional states.

Objects that are within view but are not allowed to be grabbed can cause frustration. For example, many parents with long hair find it easier to wear it up and out of reach, but even if this removes most of the temptation, your baby will still need to learn that grabbing and pulling hair is not acceptable. Fortunately, this age of impulsivity also comes with an ability to respond to the expressed emotions of others. During these times, the best thing that you can do is to remain calm, use a firm and disapproving tone of voice, and physically separate your baby from the object of interest. Follow this boundary setting by redirecting him to a different, permitted activity.

Milestones

- **Expresses a variety of emotions:** Your baby can confidently express a wide variety of emotions and expects you to acknowledge them. You may hear shrieks, coos, squeals, and wails that come along with more emphatic facial muscle movement.
- **Examines images in mirrors:** Your baby will not be able to make the association between his body and his images of self in a mirror, but inspecting reflections will become serious business and an enjoyable part of playtime.
- **Responds to the expressed emotions of others:** The faces of family will remain the most important, but your baby may now be responding to the emotional states of anyone in proximity. Hearing a shout of joy may elicit a smile, and listening to another baby cry may cause curiosity or distress.
- **Shows hesitance toward nonfamily members:** The baby who once loved to make eye contact with strangers and would willingly be passed around may avoid eye contact and be more inclined to cling to a family member or regular caregiver. This stranger-anxiety phase will likely get stronger over the next several months.
- **Begins testing limits:** Many babies are beginning to understand that some objects and activities are simply off-limits. Keep your redirection simple and gentle. It will take a lot of repetition before she truly understands what is and is not allowed.

Games and Activities

Mirror, Mirror

Your baby may not yet recognize who is in the mirror, but the images will be especially fascinating, so have some fun peeking.

1. Carry your baby over to a mirror where the two of you can peer at your reflections together.
2. Chant the mirror poem and smile on the last line. Point to each of your reflections as you name what you see.
3. Bringing a plush animal into the mirror image can add variety to this game as you play it again and again.

   Mirror, mirror, one, two, three
   Who is looking back at me?
   I see you!

Signing Happy

Teaching your baby some simple sign language can enhance her nonverbal expressive language skills.

1. Choose the right time for this activity—when you are feeling relaxed and genuinely joyful.
2. Sit in front of your baby so that she can easily see your face and chest.
3. With a big, genuine smile on your face, tell her that you feel happy right now and then make the sign for "happy."
4. Repeat the motion several times. When her interest wanes, it is time to stop for now.
5. Use this sign a few times every day. She will soon learn to associate it with the correct meaning. One day, you will see her making the sign back to you.

Note: Learning sign language with your baby can be very fun for both of you. If you are inspired by this activity, you might be interested in also learning the signs for other emotions, such as sad, angry, frustrated, and excited.

What Does a Face Say?

Nothing will help your baby learn emotional expression better than examining the human face.

1. Sit with your baby and share a book or set of cards containing pictures of baby faces with different emotions. For example, a baby face may convey an expression of happiness, anger, fear, or frustration.
2. Observe his response. Imitate these facial expressions yourself as the two of you examine each one.

Notes

My baby expresses happiness when . . .

_____

_____

_____

_____

_____

_____

_____

_____

My baby expresses sadness when . . .

_____

_____

_____

_____

_____

_____

_____

_____

MONTH

8

Your Baby This Month

Babies are still extremely dependent, but they are also experimenting with various levels of independence and self-awareness. It is no coincidence that at about the same time your baby becomes more mobile and acquires more communication skills, a new, more socially cautious behavior arises. He is also continuing to take in sensory experiences and is working hard to understand them.

Challenges This Month

- **Testing limits:** It's a normal part of childhood. The job of those grabbing fingers is to test out cause and effect. Your job is to help your little one learn which behaviors are acceptable and which are not.
- **Babysitters:** Leaving your child with a sitter may cause more tension. Allow extra time for introductions, and when you leave, make sure to convey a positive attitude, say a quick good-bye, and depart with confidence (see "Saying Bye-Bye" on page 79). He may cry, but this expression of emotion will likely stop soon after your departure.
- **Tasting the world:** It's not just toys, it's the whole world your baby will want to lick. Be on the lookout for safety and sanitary issues.

Highlights This Month

- **Peekaboo:** Your baby is starting to understand the concept of object permanence—that something out of sight can still exist. Peekaboo is the perfect game to reinforce the concept.
- **Sign language:** Teaching your baby a few signs can alleviate some of the frustration that comes with the uncomfortable period of high-receptive but low-expressive language skills. Sign language also helps develop gross motor movements, memory, and hand coordination.

Motor Skills

The wiggles and bounces from the past several months have been building the muscular strength necessary to resist gravity, sit up steadily, and make some big moves toward and away from different areas of a room. Even if babies are not crawling at this point, many are experimenting with a variety of locomotion methods, including scooting, spinning, bottom shuffling, slithering, and rolling around.

Make sure your baby has a large enough space for all of this gross motor work. If you don't see signs of crawling, don't stress. Learning to crawl usually happens within the next few months, and some never crawl at all, instead settling on other effective methods of getting from place A to place B.

Your baby's fine motor skills are continuing to progress at a good clip. The fine motor movements your baby engages in are more purposeful and more effective at picking up, transferring, and replacing small objects.

Milestones

- **Scoots in all directions:** Your baby may have found easy mobility even without crawling by scooting around with their arms and legs, backward, forward, and in a spinning motion. Some merely experiment hesitantly while others speed around.
- **Shuffles:** Not all babies scoot or crawl. Some master a sweet new move by lifting up and shuffling forward on their bottoms. Others use a tripod move with two arms and one leg pushing off, with the other leg curled under.
- **Rocks back and forth:** Rocking back and forth on all fours is a precursor to crawling, which may typically begin anytime between eight and eleven months. This lunging motion helps strengthen muscles needed for crawling.
- **Picks up small objects with four fingers and thumb:** The clawlike motion your baby uses to pick up and transfer small objects may be more purposeful and effective now. Rather than using a palm-first grabbing motion, the fingers separate and extend, subtly testing for the firmest hold. Most babies primarily use this grasp through the ninth month.

Games and Activities

Egg in a Cup

A pretend chicken egg is the perfect size for your baby's grasping hands. For this activity, you will need a wooden or plastic egg and a traditional egg cup (sold at kitchen stores) or a small, unbreakable cup that holds the egg upright.

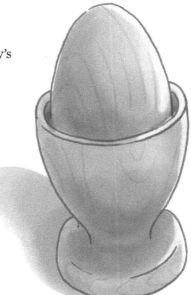

1. Place the egg inside the cup and set it in front of your baby.
2. Demonstrate how to grasp the top of the egg with your fingers and thumb and lift it into and out of the cup.
3. Allow him time to explore. If he can't yet fit the egg back inside the cup, this is a good activity to repeat later.

A Carton of Surprises

This activity makes use of an egg carton, which provides spots for picking up objects and taking them out.

1. Inside an egg carton designed to fit a dozen eggs, place six objects roughly the size of an egg at random inside six of the spots. For example, you may use pretend eggs or alphabet blocks.
2. Place the closed carton in front of your baby during playtime. Open the container and show her how to take an object out of the container.
3. Allow your baby time to work with her hand to remove all of the objects from the egg carton.

Note: The objects may end up being dumped out or shaken, and that is a perfectly acceptable variation.

Music Box

Encourage your baby to scoot or crawl by placing a musical object across the room.

1. While your baby is playing on the floor, place a music box across the room and turn the crank so that it begins to play.
2. Encourage him to focus on the music box by sitting close to it and actively listening yourself.
3. Observe as he begins to make his way toward the sound. If he is a little frustrated, remember that this is not necessarily a bad thing. You are providing a little bit of motivation to help develop those gross motor skills.

Note: If your baby becomes so frustrated that he is in real distress, soothe his emotions with a cuddle or a distraction. Try this activity again later, perhaps when he is feeling more rested, or even in a few weeks after you see more progress toward scooting and crawling.

Sensory Development

Working out the spatial relationships between oneself and objects is serious business. Your little explorer is likely to be putting both mouth and fingers onto every available surface for immediate gratification. While your child is the curious one, you are the guide. She is following your gaze to the objects you focus on and internalizing and imitating your shifts in body language. She is analyzing and committing to memory every worldly item you expose her to repeatedly.

To counteract the intensity of this stage, make sure that your baby has plenty of sensory experiences available for exploration throughout the day. To keep her engaged without being overstimulated, consider storing most of her toys and rotating the selection throughout the week.

Milestones

- **Recognizes people and objects from across the room:** Visual skills are almost adultlike, around 20/40. Your baby may not be able to reach the items on a high shelf or the artwork or photos on the walls around your home, but they are a form of eye candy. When you are gazing with her out at a landscape, the objects in the distance will still be a little blurry.
- **Follows your gaze if you look away:** Your baby's vision is adept enough to quickly assess which direction you are looking in and hunt for the item that might be capturing your interest.
- **Categorizes physical properties of objects:** Your baby is beginning to remember that different objects have distinct properties when manipulated. Round things roll. Flat things slide. Rubbery things grip. Tags can be pulled. Manipulating objects to discover and categorize these properties is a priority.
- **Discerns different tactile sensations:** Textured objects have always been appealing, but your baby is likely to be fascinated with all of the minor details. Offering contrasting sensory experiences will help her understand the similarities and differences between them, such as exploring rough and smooth, warm and cold, and soft and coarse.
- **Enthusiastically makes noise:** The joy of a baby's face while beating a drum, a pot, or even a watermelon cannot be underestimated. She is thoroughly enjoying hands-on musical and movement activities.

Games and Activities

Rough and Smooth

Intentionally offering isolated experiences with different textures helps develop your baby's sense of touch. This is an activity you can do anywhere and at any time. Try using trees or other outdoor natural materials to give rough-versus-smooth experiences.

1. Go for a walk outside with your baby and find a natural material that is rough, such as tree bark.
2. Say the word "rough." Allow him to fully explore the rough surface with his fingers (not his mouth unless you have verified the surface to be safe).
3. Hunt for a natural material that is smooth, such as a large stone, to explore in contrast.
4. Say the word "smooth." Allow him to fully explore this new object with his fingers.

Pots 'n' Pans

This joyful noisemaking activity is a classic.

1. Sit down with your baby on the floor and provide both a wooden spoon and a pot turned upside down.
2. Rather than showing him exactly how to bang on the pot, demonstrate how to pick up the wooden spoon and hold it by the handle.
3. Allow him to explore with the two items and discover the noise that can be made by banging the spoon on the pot.
4. If he has mastered the basic pot and spoon, vary the equipment by providing different sizes of pots and different kitchen tools for musical exploration.

Warm and Cold

Offer the opportunity for your baby to experience both warmth and coldness using two washcloths, preferably of the same color.

1. Place one washcloth under cold running water. Wring it out and set it aside. Alternatively, place a wet washcloth in the refrigerator for ten minutes.
2. Place another washcloth under slightly warm running water. Wring it out and set it aside.
3. Now offer both washcloths to your baby and allow her to explore them with her fingers and mouth.
4. Sit back and observe. Does she seem to notice the temperature difference? Does she prefer one item over another?

Language and Mental Development

Both words and gestures are becoming more significant for your baby. You might notice her perking up and looking for a person or object when you say familiar words, like a family member's name or that of a favorite toy. Since object permanence is solidifying around this time, your baby begins to understand that the world is fairly constant. The things you talk about may not be visible, but they are still around somewhere. The word "no" is also taking on an extra special meaning as well.

Many babies are able to use sign language and other common gestures that convey specific meanings. It can be a thrill to communicate with your baby in this way, and it can also ease frustration over the next few months. You may have heard that using sign language can cause a speech delay. Leave your worries at the door, because there is growing evidence that this is not a problem as long as you keep talking to your little one. Some babies will babble frequently, and others will be more on the quiet side, and that's just personality. Either way, keep on chatting.

Milestones

- **Understands "no" more clearly:** As your baby experiments with cause and effect and finds that you are setting certain limits on undesirable activities, the meaning of the word "no" will become clearer. Now he may pause and look at you first for confirmation before testing to see if your no from yesterday still means no today. Be consistent.
- **Waves bye-bye:** With a little practice, when you say "bye-bye," your baby may quickly learn that these words go with a special movement: a hand wave. Strangers and loved ones are likely to respond with enthusiasm to this expressive motion, providing lots of positive reinforcement.
- **Interprets gestures:** The connection between movement and meaning is becoming more distinct. Your baby is becoming more proficient at remembering that when you make a certain motion, such as if you use the sign for "more," there is a specific result that happens immediately afterward, such as extra food appearing.
- **Combines different sounds together:** The babbling continues, and new sounds may be combined. For example, previously your baby may have been repeating same-sound beginning consonant syllables such as "da-da-da-da" but now might be babbling different beginning consonant syllables, such as "ba-da-ba-da."

- **Looks for you or dropped toys:** When you leave the room, your baby is beginning to understand that you still exist, even if she can't see you at the moment. This cognitive concept of object permanence is in full play, and it's a delightful realization for her to discover that a hidden object still exists. Her memory for where objects belong is getting stronger.

Games and Activities

Object Permanence Box

A toy that disappears and reappears demonstrates the concept of object permanence.

1. To prepare, you need a small cardboard box and a ball. Cut a hole in the top of the box just big enough for the ball to fit through and a large opening at the bottom edge of one of the sides for the ball to roll out.
2. Show your baby how to put the ball into the hole. Thanks to natural momentum, the ball usually rolls out of the large opening on its own. If it does not, reach inside to retrieve the ball.
3. Offer the ball to your baby and ask, "Would you like to put the ball inside?" Give her another turn and continue as long as she's interested.

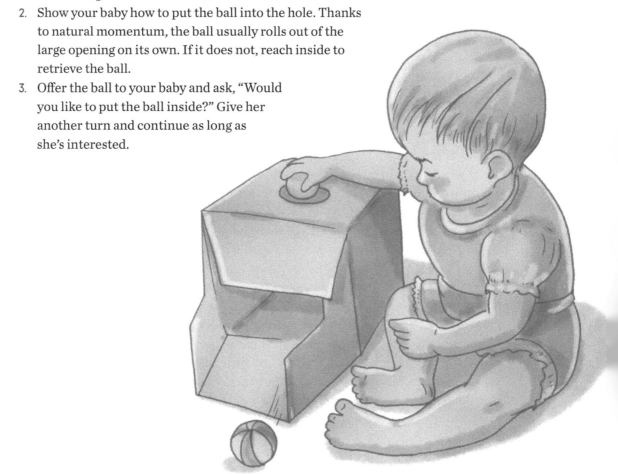

A First Fort

Create a hiding place to show your baby that you still exist, even if you move out of sight, demonstrating object permanence. Practicing waving good-bye develops social skills and helps attach meaning to an action.

1. Put a blanket over a sturdy table to create a fort, leaving an opening large enough for your baby to crawl through.
2. Sit down next to her beside the fort. Say "bye-bye" and wave, then crawl inside where she can't see you.
3. If your baby is mobile, wait a few moments to see if she comes to find you. If not, peek out and say hello.
4. Repeat this activity several times, as long as she is interested.

THE DEAL WITH DIRT

Whether hanging out at the park or in the living room, it's harder to keep things sanitary with your baby's increased mobility. She probably won't mind eating a bit of dirt now and then, and fortunately exposure to some dirt is fairly harmless.

A sensible approach when it comes to dirt is to balance sensory exploration with basic cleanliness, along with your safety assessment of the surrounding environment. If you have concerns, adjust what your child can access accordingly or go somewhere else.

There's no need to panic if you see your baby eating something picked up off the floor or the ground outside. Since mouthing objects is still one of the main ways she learns about the world, maintain a calm and positive attitude as you help her learn what is safe and what is not.

More

All Done

Signing "More" and "All Done"

The signs for "more" and "all done" can help you better understand when your baby is thoroughly enjoying a food or activity and when to move on to something else—without the typical frustration.

1. Choose the right time for this activity. Many parents find that feeding solid foods offers many opportunities to practice these signs.
2. Sit in front of your baby so that your face and chest can be easily seen.
3. With an exaggerated questioning look on your face, ask if he would like more while you make the sign for "more." Offer him more of the food or offer to repeat an activity at this point.
4. When you sense that he is finished eating or the activity is over, make the sign for "all done" and say, "You look like you're all done. You're finished."
5. Continue using these signs whenever appropriate. Your baby will spontaneously begin imitating you and then initiating these signs. That is when you will know that the meaning is setting in.

Social-Emotional Skills

Your baby is a willing participant in your social world and may have picked up many of the subtle gestures and habits that you take for granted as an adult. From greeting everyone with a smile to hugs just for loved ones, your baby is a social creature beginning to understand that she is part of a community. Every society has guidelines for behavior, so she is learning what is and is not acceptable. This requires a lot of testing to figure out where the limits are.

This realization comes because babies are just now realizing that they are separate people with their own thoughts, feelings, wishes, and frustrations. They can even scoot toward or away from their caregivers. It can be scary to acquire this new independence, so babies have developed a defensive response system to ensure their survival. By clinging to you and protesting when you leave, they are letting you know that you are still very much needed to provide food, protection, and love.

Milestones

- **Experiences separation anxiety:** The hesitance you glimpsed earlier when your baby was around strangers may have grown into full-blown anxiety. Some babies have a more intense bout than others. With consistent, loving reassurance (see "Saying Bye-Bye" on page 79), this phase will pass in its own time.
- **Tests boundaries impulsively:** Expect that even when you have redirected your baby or said no in the past, he may insist on repeating the disallowed behavior. Having boundaries is a new and somewhat exhilarating experience. Since he lacks the ability to use logic to understand why the boundary is there, you must be very consistent so that your baby accepts that the boundary does indeed exist.
- **Uses vocalizations and gestures to get attention:** Your baby is starting to become more selective about the most effective methods to get your attention. You might see him trying out a variety of attention-getting techniques. He will note the ones that work for later use.
- **Objects if you try to take a toy away:** With the new awareness of self versus others comes the knowledge that a person can possess an item. If you try to take a toy or other object away before your baby has finished playing with it, this action may elicit a big cry of frustration.
- **Greets people with a smile:** It may be brief or bashful, but your baby knows that the proper acknowledgment of a person requires a smile. Since birth, this is the way other people have greeted him, and now this social expectation is understood and performed on cue.

Games and Activities

I'll Be Back

A bit of practice can make separation a little easier for both of you.

1. While your baby is playing in a familiar place, give your baby a hug and a kiss and say, "I'm going to get something, but I'll be back."
2. Wave bye-bye.
3. Step out of the room for a few seconds, but if your little one is stressing about it, come right back.
4. Repeat this activity now and again to reinforce her knowledge that you will always return.

Make New Friends

You will need a friend or relative who hasn't spent a lot of time with your baby to help you with this activity. While your baby has obviously met strangers in the past, it's a different kind of challenge at this age, when she may be less receptive to new people due to separation anxiety.

1. Sit down with your baby in a familiar place and have another person sit a few feet away from the two of you. Make sure this person knows not to touch your baby during this exercise.
2. Introduce your baby to the other person with comforting words. For example, you might say something such as, "This is Julie. She's my friend. She's nice."
3. Over the next several minutes, ask your friend to scoot closer and closer toward your baby while the two of you talk.
4. If your baby seems comfortable, walk across the room to retrieve an item, and then walk back to sit with her again.
5. Give your friend a toy to offer to her while you go to a different part of the room.
6. Simply observe and respect your baby's reactions. If she seems comfortable, you can try stepping out of the room for a few minutes, but stop at any sign of distress and comfort her.

Be with You

When your baby is in a clingy mood, offer empathy and reassure him with cuddles and a song.

1. Lift your baby up and hold him close. Kiss his soft baby cheek. Breathe deeply and nuzzle his head just like you may have done when he was a newborn.
2. Say, "I love you soooooo much."
3. Now sing the "Be with You" song. You can make up your own tune or sing it to the tune of "Skip to my Lou." Sway, twirl, and bounce while you sing.
4. When the song is over, kiss your little one again and say, "I love you soooooo much. I love to be with you."

All I want is to be with you,
Play and sing and cuddle, too.
All I want is to be with you,
Be with you all day.

We can go up, and we can go down,
We can go all around the town,
But all I want is to be with you,
Be with you all day.

Notes

Here's how my baby gets around this month:

_____

_____

_____

_____

_____

_____

_____

Some of the boundaries my baby is testing are . . .

_____

_____

_____

_____

_____

_____

_____

_____

MONTH

9

Your Baby This Month

If you could take a peek inside your baby's brain, you would be shocked at all of the new bits of knowledge swimming about. Those neurons are making rapid-fire connections that will pave the way for new skills. Some are essential for survival, such as learning how to pick up, chew, and swallow solid foods. Others ensure physical independence, such as pulling up to stand. There are also words and gestures to learn and practice that support essential social skills, such as saying the names of loved ones and clapping to express joy. You may even get a hug from your sweetie.

The ninth month brings big changes in expressive capabilities and independence. There may be times when you feel like you cannot provide enough stimulation or attention to satisfy your baby's more-more-more attitude, and there may be times when you feel that he has plateaued on certain skills and is lacking motivation to progress. Patience is your friend.

Challenges This Month

- **Frustrations:** *Wait, the world is not entirely free for me to explore?* This realization may come as a shock to your baby, who was used to having free rein to explore within the natural limits of his motor skills.
- **Staying safe:** The advances in new motor skills have given your baby the ability to grab faster and pull harder. Your baby has no way to tell what's safe and what's not, so babyproofing becomes even more important.
- **Feeling secure:** Separation anxiety is still affecting your baby's ability to enjoy her newfound independence. You may find that she is more insistent on staying near you at all times. Many babies develop an attachment to comfort objects as well.

Highlights This Month

- **Self-feeding:** Whether using the fingers in a clawlike motion or developing a more refined pincer grasp, most babies are intrigued by the idea of self-feeding and will attempt to pick up and move food into their mouths.
- **New motor skills:** Some babies are holding on to a raised surface and pulling up to a stand. Other babies are perfecting the art of crawling over obstacles. Expect new and exciting developments, and understand that before any big burst of development often comes a slight regression or plateau.
- **Encouragement:** Your baby is working hard and looking to you for emotional support and a positive attitude about his hard work. As he accomplishes new things, he's feeling the intrinsic reward and satisfaction from his efforts paying off.

Motor Skills

Crawling and pulling to a stand can be a joyful and liberating experience. As cute as it is, the classic baby crawl isn't necessary for every baby. Some babies continue or perfect alternate methods, such as scooting, slithering, or shuffling instead, and then go on to pulling up and standing. These are perfectly normal developmental progressions.

Your baby's personality also influences his level of activity. Some babies are simply more content to sit and hang out, and others are scrambling as quickly as they can to reach a toy on the other side of the room. Remember that your baby may be a few months ahead of these major motor milestones or a few months behind, and that is normal. These timelines are just general guides, so don't let them stress you out if your baby isn't quite there yet.

Milestones

- **Crawls:** Those little arms and legs are finding their groove, and this month or the next is when most babies figure out that cross crawling, using the opposite arm and leg at the same time, is an effective method for self-transportation. Some babies never crawl using this method, instead choosing other ways to get around, so don't worry if yours does not master this milestone and instead goes right into standing and walking.
- **Pulls up to stand:** Sometime in this month or in the next, most babies learn how to reach up to a low, stable surface and pull up to a stand. While her upper and lower body strength may not be developed enough to hold this position for long, many babies are able to stand up for brief periods.
- **Bangs objects together with two hands:** Since your baby's grip is firmer and the two hands are more coordinated, she may be able to reliably bring them together in sync to bang toys or other objects together and repeat this motion.
- **Drops objects on purpose:** Gravity is fascinating, and if your baby is in a high chair, she may intentionally drop food or a spoon and watch its descent. She's learning by experimenting.

Games and Activities

The Pull-up Place

To encourage your baby to pull up to a standing position from a sitting position, provide a pull-up place: a low wooden bar hung securely on the wall, an ottoman, or a sturdy stool approximately 17 inches high, positioned so that it won't slide. To spur interest in this area, place an unbreakable, securely attached mirror nearby, for example directly behind the wooden bar on the wall.

1. If your baby is already attempting to pull up to a stand, sit with her on the ground in front of the pull-up place.
2. Say, "I wonder if you'd like to stand up."
3. For the first use, support your baby's hips and offer gentle assistance as she rises from a seated position and reaches for the pull-up place. Show your baby where to put her hands if needed.
4. Continue to sit next to her and offer support sitting back down, if it is needed.
5. From here on out, she may remember that this is the pull-up place and may move toward this place when interested in pulling up. Allow her the time and space to work on this skill independently.

Note: Make sure all wall attachments, such as wooden bars or mirrors, are properly and securely installed. Never use a regular glass mirror that could shatter. Instead, source an unbreakable childcare mirror intended for this use.

WORDS OF ENCOURAGEMENT

When it comes to mastering skills, your baby depends on you to give emotional support. He's relying on your warm, loving connection and positive attitude toward hard work—especially when a task feels difficult to overcome or a little scary.

It may surprise you, but for most children, the intrinsic reward that comes with accomplishment is enough. No praise is necessary—in fact, research shows that it can actually backfire if it focuses on a child's abilities and accomplishments, rather than his effort. Here are a few tips for offering encouragement.

Use your face: Your baby is acutely attuned to the expressions on your face. Right from the beginning he has been looking into your eyes for guidance. If he looks a little insecure or anxious, make sure your expression is relaxed and reassuring. This will show him that you are confident in his abilities.

Observe and describe: Take the time to watch the exact motions your baby is making and comment on what you see. Focus on the effort. For example, if your baby is on the verge of crawling, you might say, "You are reaching farther each time. You really seem to want to get over to that toy. You're working so hard to get there."

Be specific and sincere: It's easy to fall into a habit of saying "good job" automatically in response to everything your child does. Instead, comment specifically and sincerely on what your child is doing right now. Stay focused on the process, not the end result.

Rocking Rings

Exploring a toy ring stacker with a rocking base will help your baby develop hand-eye coordination.

1. Remove all of the rings that go with the stacker except for the largest.
2. Sit with your baby and slowly demonstrate how to remove one ring and replace it.
3. Allow him time to fully explore this toy.
4. Offer more rings as he expresses interest in performing this activity.

Over and Under

Create an indoor obstacle course for your crawling baby.

1. Set a safe and stable piece of furniture, such as a wooden chair, and a few pillows to serve as obstacles in a space where your baby has room to crawl, such as in the middle of a room or in a hallway.
2. Switch around the placement and add variety as your baby becomes more adept at navigating the obstacles. Consider adding a play tunnel.

Sensory Development

All of the senses are well developed, allowing your baby to take minor calculated risks. As strong as separation anxiety may be during these last few months of the first year, for many babies it is a very brave age as well.

Milestones

- **Enjoys tasting different foods:** Your baby may enthusiastically sample different foods this month and explore textures with his tongue—for example, foods that contrast with one another, such as sweet and sour, bland and spicy, or grainy and smooth.
- **Feeds self with fingers:** With the fingers and thumb working better in sync and getting stronger, your baby is able to feed herself small chunks of food about the size of a blueberry. In fact, blueberries can be an excellent food to practice this skill. Scattering chunks of food on your baby's tray or plate helps him see where each piece is and aim for them with intention.

- **Becomes more aware of heights:** All of the gross motor skills your baby has been practicing are helping further increase depth perception. This is important because along with crawling, pulling up, and cruising comes the possibility that your baby will be more cautious when encountering an obstacle or surface drop.
- **Quickly identifies faces and objects:** Not only can your baby see clearly from fairly far away, but she is also constantly scanning for facial features and items encountered previously. She alerts you with excitement or trepidation using gestures and vocalizations.
- **Concentrates when hearing banging and shaking sounds:** The enthusiasm for making noise continues. Your baby perks up his ears especially for the sounds he makes himself.

Games and Activities

Pot and Block

To reinforce object permanence and the concepts of in and out, all you need is a large metal pot, a metal lid, and a wooden block or other small toy.

1. Place the block inside the pot and cover the pot with the lid. Lower the pot to the floor.
2. Sit next to your baby and say, "I wonder what's in there."
3. Demonstrate lifting the lid up slowly and expressing surprise at what you see inside.
4. Take the block out of the pot and examine it with curiosity. Then hold it up above the pot and drop it back in. Listen intently for the clunk. Replace the lid.
5. Now allow your baby to explore. He may repeat your actions or may be more interested in putting the lid on and off, and that is just fine. Follow your baby's lead here.

Shake It Big

A large sealed container can be repurposed for some noisy fun.

1. Fill your large container with one cup of popcorn kernels or dried beans. Secure the lid tightly so that it cannot be opened.
2. Sit next to your baby in front of the container. Demonstrate how to pick up the container, slowly tilt it from side to side, and shake it once or twice vigorously with two hands. Slowly return it to the floor.
3. Observe her as she explores the container. Put the container away when you're done.

A Tasting Plate

Developing taste buds crave new textures. Help your child learn to discriminate between types of food by offering two at one time.

1. On your baby's plate, put a small sample of two foods your baby enjoys eating that have very different textures. For example, put a small piece of strawberry on one side of the plate and a tiny piece of broccoli on the other.
2. Invite him to independently try these foods. He will use the pincer grasp to pick them up and place them into his mouth.
3. Observe your baby's reactions. Does his facial expression change from one food to the other as he chews? Does his body language change?

Language and Mental Development

Yes, now when your baby says your name, it's really all about you. This development is a delight for a parent who has been waiting to hear "mama" or "dada." Expressing complex thoughts and feelings is still quite a ways off, but your baby's receptive skills are likely to be noticeably improving day by day. When you ask her to go get a ball that's across the room, she is likely to know the word "ball," hunt for the ball, and then crawl, shuffle, or scoot toward it.

Nursery rhymes and games such as fingerplays and peekaboo are favorites. Don't be surprised, however, if your baby seems to lose interest quickly and wants to move on to the next thing. Most babies at eight and nine months old have short attention spans for a reason: They are mentally hungry for new experiences and can feel frustrated by their physical limitations.

You don't need to invest in a bunch of new toys, which is only a short-term fix, as most babies cast off the new ones just as quickly. Instead, try rotating the toys more frequently and storing the rest out of sight so that they become new again next time you take them out. As she gains more mobility and dexterity, you are likely to see an increase in the ability to self-entertain.

Milestones

- **Recognizes and responds to familiar words:** Your baby's receptive language skills are advancing quickly now. Many babies regularly respond to their own names and those of family members. They also respond well to words that go with favorite toys and familiar routines, with vocalizations, gestures, and actions.
- **Verbalizes a few words with meaning:** Your baby may have acquired a few favorite words to practice saying. By now, the way she communicates with you nonverbally indicates that the meaning of these words is also solid. For many, it begins with "mama" or "dada" and then expands to other favorite people, objects, or pets.
- **Laughs appropriately:** When your baby giggles, it may be much more intentional and in the moment. Laughing is a way to share a humorous experience with other people. Simple rhymes and games often naturally have consistently funny parts that you can repeat as you play together. Remember, babies love repetition!
- **Searches longer for desired toys:** Object permanence is becoming more established, and your baby may not give up as easily when she can't find an object she wants, such as a favorite toy that's usually in the same basket with other toys.

Games and Activities

Helicopter

Take your baby on a helicopter tour of some familiar digs as you keep up a steady stream of narration for vocabulary development.

1. Create a forward-facing "chair" for your baby with one arm securely underneath your baby's bottom and the other arm securing his chest against your own. Your baby should now be able to look out as you carry him. An alternate position for this is the hip carry, where your baby faces in toward you, hugging your hip with his legs while you put your hand around his back.
2. Ask your baby if he would like to take a helicopter ride. If your baby seems up for it, say, "Helicopter is taking off." Make a "putta-putta" sound as you begin to walk around the house.
3. Be your baby's tour guide, narrating as you go, just like you might imagine on a show about traveling to a tourist destination. For example, "Just beyond the bend, we can see the refrigerator. This keeps our food cold and fresh. Now we're swooping in low to take in the view of the dishwasher."
4. When you reach your final destination, make the "putta-putta" sound again and lower your baby back to the ground.

Dancing Feet

This funny game is especially useful as a transition song if you're putting on a pair of booties.

1. Sit your baby in your lap and lightly hold her ankles, one in each hand.
2. Gently shake one foot, then the other foot, and then both feet, alternating with each line as you chant the poem.

Footsie and Wootsie dance around
Footsie and Wootsie touch the ground
Footsie and Wootsie jump and hop
Footsie and Wootsie run, then stop

FINDING COMFORT IN OBJECTS

Plush animals, blankies, and more: Is your baby showing signs of attachment? Not all babies do, but developing an emotional connection to a familiar object is very common from 8 to 12 months. This comforting item, often called a transitional object, soothes separation anxiety, and many babies won't want to leave the house without theirs. Having a healthy attachment to an object can aid your baby by allowing for easier transitions from the home into the car seat, into the care of a babysitter, or even while you are performing regular household chores and your baby is having playtime nearby.

Most parents would prefer that this object be small, washable, and easily replaceable, but since children are unique individuals, you never know what your child may become attached to. As long as it is safe and not a choking hazard, you can cater to your child's wishes and allow your child to carry around this item from place to place.

Cabinet Surprise

Open the door and peek in. What will you find inside? Is it still there when you close the cabinet door?

1. For a fun surprise, secretly place a plush animal or other toy inside a cabinet that is available for opening and closing. Make sure that all items in this cabinet are baby-safe.
2. Sit in front of the cabinet door with your baby and say, "I wonder what's inside. Let's find out." Assist your baby in opening the door and look inside together.
3. Exclaim surprise at the toy you find. After your baby examines the toy, place it back inside the cabinet and close the door again.
4. Now peek back in to see if it's still in there.

Note: This game is fun to repeat with a different object every time you play it.

Social-Emotional Skills

Social situations are becoming ever more intriguing to your baby, who now realizes that there could be a part to play in every scene. After months of observation, your baby may be pointing at objects to start "conversations," clapping on cue, hugging loved ones, and waving bye-bye with fair regularity. If there is an opportunity to engage in a one-on-one interaction or community ritual (like applause), your baby is more willing to give it a try.

Frustration levels could also be ramping up at this time, as your baby starts to understand more clearly that access to some of the world's most curious objects, such as eyeglasses or electrical cords, is firmly off-limits. The feelings of "but it's not fair" will persist for years, as children do not have the prefrontal cortex development to tap in to logic and reason. Your baby's boundaries will need to be extremely consistent and regularly enforced with a no-nonsense but empathetic tone of voice.

Milestones

*   **Points at objects:** That pudgy little finger may be pointing everywhere and at everyone this month. Consider it a sign that your baby is expressing an interest and is using this physical method to start a conversation.

- **Claps hands to express joy:** Your baby may be showing you a lot of excitement through clapping this month, and the act of putting two hands together to make some noise in a social setting is very good for physical and emotional development.
- **Tests limits and observes parental reactions:** Just because you have set a limit on a certain unsafe or destructive behavior does not mean that your baby will follow it. He may be testing you to see if you mean what you say, and also because it is safe to practice risk-taking with an adult who is trusted and beloved.
- **Expresses frustration at restrictions:** As a parent, it is your job to make sure that your little one is protected from harm and that the objects your baby plays with are treated with respect. Some of the restrictions may be very frustrating since she is not able to understand why you are prohibiting her freedom to explore.
- **Shows physical affection:** If you have been cuddling and hugging since birth, now is the time when you are likely to see some of those affections returned with intention. Other family members may be the happy recipients of gentle squeezes and pats.

Games and Activities

Hugs for Everyone

Giving a hug takes bravery and practice. Role-play this skill together.

1. While your baby is watching, demonstrate how to give a hug to someone you love.
2. Ask the other person if she would like a hug. If the answer is yes, show your baby how to wrap your arms around the other person gently. Then move apart again.
3. Ask your baby if she would like to also give that person a hug. If she does not, accept the response without added pressure.
4. Continue modeling hugging whenever you see an appropriate opportunity. You can hug dolls or plush animals, too.

It's Fun to Celebrate

Everybody likes to party sometimes. Clap your hands and celebrate just for the fun of it.

1. Sit in front of your baby and make eye contact, with a big smile on your face. This would be a great time to make the sign for "happy" (see page 108).
2. Now begin to clap your hands in rhythm while you chant this poem. Instead of "baby," substitute your little one's name to personalize the experience.
3. When you get to the word "hooray," throw your arms up high in the air and shake your hands.

4. Allow your baby to observe. With enough repetition over time, you may see your baby imitating your movements.

Two, four, six, eight,
It's Baby's turn to celebrate.
Hooray!

Pointing Walk

That little index finger may be pointing everywhere once this skill is learned. Embrace it and go for a walk to introduce vocabulary words as you point.

1. Carry your baby around the house to look around together.
2. Pause inside every room to point out three items of interest.
3. Ask "What do we see in here?" If your baby points to an item, you might say, "You're pointing at the lamp."
4. If your baby doesn't take the initiative, model the pointing yourself. For example, you might say, "I see the lamp. I'm pointing at the lamp."

Notes

This month, my baby enjoys pointing or looking at . . .

_____

_____

_____

_____

_____

_____

This month, my baby is frustrated when . . .

_____

_____

_____

_____

_____

_____

MONTH

10

Your Baby This Month

Your little one has been growing outside of the womb for about as long as a typical pregnancy. And just look at the vast amount of growth that has happened during that time! You now have an inquisitive and communicative family member with original thoughts, feelings, and ideas to share with the world.

Flexibility and mobility have taken another big leap. Getting around from place to place, manipulating intriguing objects, and even a menu of favorite foods isn't so tough anymore. In fact, it might feel so easy to crawl off to play independently that your baby has, in response, become even more attached to you and aware of your presence. This is a natural instinct for protection. She will be instinctively trying all kinds of new things, and some of those will be a little risky. Keeping a parent close by just makes sense from her perspective. Now is the time to teach her what foods are good to eat, what toys are safe to play with, and how to have a back-and-forth conversation.

Challenges This Month

- **Playgroup playtime:** Taking your baby to a playgroup can be a fun and helpful experience for both of you, but it has some challenges. Babies of this age don't actually play together; they play parallel to each other, and they may be upset when a toy is grabbed away.
- **Bumps and bruises:** If your baby is pulling up on furniture or crawling fairly quickly, you may see some bruises appear after a tumble. Common places for bumps and bruises include the forehead, elbows, knees, and shins.
- **New fears:** Aside from the separation anxiety that is so common, your baby may suddenly become fearful of familiar sounds and objects. Common new fears include the vacuum cleaner, the toilet flushing, and barking dogs. For most children, this is temporary. Try to remain calm and comforting, but don't overreact or force your child to have a close encounter with the source of these troubled emotions. These worries typically subside on their own.

Highlights This Month

- **First words:** Some babies are saying a first word or two this month, and that is something that many parents like to record and remember with fondness later on.
- **Copycat games:** Back-and-forth vocalizations and movements are hugely appealing to most babies. Get your silly on, because your baby will enjoy being your mirror and letting you do the imitating, too.
- **Messy play:** Self-feeding alone provides plenty of opportunities for messy play, but your baby also might enjoy feeling the squishy mud outdoors or crawling through a pile of leaves. Whatever you do, don't shy away from sensory experiences because of a possible mess. It's a developmentally appropriate part of your baby's education.

Motor Skills

Keeping up with your baby may feel like trying to chase a rolling ball down a hill. Many babies will not be afraid in the least to aim and lunge for exactly what they want to explore, and once they get there, they may quickly move along to the next enticing thing. Fortunately, the motor skills your baby has been practicing for the last nine months are being put to good use, and your baby is likely practicing switching from one type of movement to the other on a whim.

Entertaining your little ball of energy doesn't need to be difficult. Make sure that you are keeping floor space open for big movements and providing a regular rotation of interesting objects to manipulate. The fine motor skills are continuing to develop just as quickly as the gross motor skills. Babies tend to be especially interested in pinching, pulling, and letting go of objects.

Milestones

- **Switches positions:** From sitting to crawling to pulling up, then back to sitting and craning over sideways, babies are learning to change body positions impulsively with much less effort than before.
- **Pulls to a stand and balances:** By the end of this month, many babies are pulling up to a stand, and some are even able to stand alone unsupported for a few seconds. Cruising is also a possibility either now or in the near future, as your baby is looking for surfaces to hold on to for support in learning to walk.
- **Refines the pincer grip:** Your baby may be making more attempts to use the thumb and index finger in coordination to pick up tiny objects, a skill that eases self-feeding. Most one-year-olds have mastered this skill.
- **Manipulates objects:** Those busy little fingers are working hard to effect change on objects. You might notice that your baby is exploring how to open and close, push and pull, twist and turn all kinds of objects. The primary purpose is practicing fine motor skills and exploring the properties, not necessarily using the object for its intended purpose.
- **Learns to let go voluntarily:** Up until around now, your baby's primary motivation when it came to obtaining objects was to clutch and hold it until it fell of its own accord. Last month, you might have noticed him beginning to experiment with dropping items. This month, you might be seeing more muscle control involved as he purposefully lets go of an object and observes the effect.

Games and Activities

Pinch It Up

This pinch, pull, and reveal activity will hone fine motor skills.

1. In one of your fists, lightly hold a long, thin, sturdy object, such as a straw, dowel, or unsharpened pencil. The tip of the object should point up toward the ceiling. Do not clench it so tightly that your baby cannot pull it out, but do not let it fall out of your grasp, either.
2. While your baby is watching, demonstrate the activity. With your open hand, use your index finger and thumb to pull the object up and out of your fist.
3. Now place it back into your fist and offer it to your baby to pull out. If she uses a technique other than the pincer grasp to pull it out, that is perfectly fine.

Note: If the object you are using is not safe for your baby to mouth, make sure to monitor closely and put the object away when you are done.

The Ribbon Trick

Your baby may be delighted when the ribbon pulling seems to never end, which is perfect for strengthening that pincer grip.

1. Tie together several two-foot-long ribbons and place them loosely in a small box or plastic container with a small hole cut out of the lid. For example, you might use a tissue box or a large yogurt container.
2. Poke the open end of the first ribbon out of the hole.
3. Demonstrate for your baby how to tug on the ribbon using your index finger and thumb so that it pulls out of the hole a bit.
4. Allow your baby to explore various methods of pulling. If your baby does not use the pincer grip to pull it out, that is perfectly okay. This game is still refining fine motor skills.

Note: Put the ribbon away when you are finished. Never leave your baby with it unattended.

The Ball Tracker

Your baby will be mesmerized as he practices letting go of the ball and watching it roll all the way down to the bottom of a zigzag ramp.

1. A ball tracker is a toy you can purchase or make yourself by cutting and bending cardboard into a series of ramps that allow a ball to roll down to the bottom. Using the ball tracker, sit down with your baby in your lap as you demonstrate putting the ball down the hole at the top of the ball-tracking ramp.
2. Watch with your baby as the ball zooms down the track in a zigzag motion.
3. When the ball reaches the bottom, allow her to reach for it and grasp it.
4. Ask your baby if she would like to put the ball in the top. Assist her to a stand if needed, wait for her to drop the ball, and then sit back down quickly to watch the action.

Steady Rings

Rings have a unique shape that makes them intriguing for babies learning how to manipulate objects. For this activity, buy or assemble a structure with a large vertical peg on a stable base. You will also need a few large ring-shaped objects.

1. For your baby's first experience with this stacker, remove the rings and set them to the side.
2. Sit next to him and slowly demonstrate how to put one ring on the peg and take it off again.
3. Hand the ring to your baby and allow him time to fully explore this toy with all of the available rings.

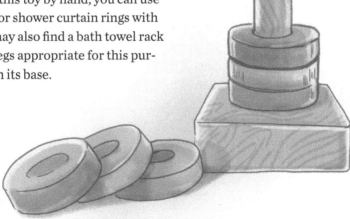

Note: If you are making this toy by hand, you can use napkin rings, bracelets, or shower curtain rings with your wooden peg. You may also find a bath towel rack or set of coat-hanging pegs appropriate for this purpose when turned flat on its base.

Sensory Development

Your little one might be poking and prodding into everything these days and dropping lots of things on the floor, too. Messy play is healthy play, but that doesn't mean you have to let it get out of your control. By restricting the number of toys or amount of food available at one time and having cleanup supplies readily available, you can usually tone down the mess to a manageable level. Babies thrive on messy sensory experiences, but they also appreciate an uncluttered, ordered space to make that mess in.

Your baby is likely to be developing a deeper ability to focus during playtime, tuning out extraneous sounds like the doorbell or people chatting in another room. You'll see those little hands becoming very, very busy as well, quickly sussing out the unique properties of every object.

Milestones

- **Feeds self with more skill:** A more refined ability to pick up tiny objects with the fingers and thumb leads to a vastly increased capability for self-feeding. Your baby might be more adept at getting food into the mouth using both utensils and fingers. Embrace the mess and plan for cleanup time at the end. More is going into her mouth than you might think.

- **Conducts purposeful sensory investigations:** Ever curious, your baby knows the drill on how to investigate toys now. You are likely to see a lot more purposeful movement as a result of her memory for the results of previous experiments: Does this ball bounce? Does this box open? What happens when I shake this?

- **Is less distracted by extraneous noises:** Being able to hear what one person is saying in a roomful of people talking is a useful skill. Distractions are much easier for babies to tune out at this age. You're likely to notice this increased ability in sustained focus and selective hearing when reading aloud to her.

- **Views objects from a distance and crawls toward them:** When your baby sees desirable objects in the distance, she will be able to gauge the distance more accurately and move to retrieve them independently. This type of independence is a confidence booster.

Games and Activities

Hoot, Hoot!

Give your baby a bottle and listen to what happens.

1. Sit down in front of your baby while holding an empty, unbreakable bottle in your hands.
2. Slowly bring it up to your mouth and make some hooting noises into it. You might try different vowel sounds such as "hoo," "bah," or "gee."
3. Offer the bottle to him and sit back patiently, allowing lots of time for exploration.

SCREEN TIME

How you choose to handle the issue of screen time is a personal choice. When it comes to educating young children, however, human-to-human interaction wins over electronics every time. In fact, the American Academy of Pediatrics recommends that children under the age of 18 months have no screen time.

Video chats are the one exception. They enable you and your baby to have back-and-forth conversation with a person who's actively engaged at the other end, like a parent traveling for work or a grandparent who lives too far away to easily visit.

Be skeptical when you're bombarded by marketing hype that espouses the educational benefits for babies of products that require screen time. Babies who watch videos or use apps do not have more developed vocabularies or other cognitive skills than babies who do not.

Bottom line: A screen cannot offer the sensory exploration and social- emotional stimulus from humans that babies need. Your baby learns best from one-on-one human interaction with lots of time playing and working on gross motor skills. Don't let electronics take time away from that.

Sock Mysteries

Repurpose mismatched socks to play this sensory discovery game.

1. Place three adult-size socks inside of a basket. Now fill each sock with a different object that has a distinctively different shape and feel.
2. Sitting next to your baby, select one of the socks to demonstrate with. Feel the weight of it in your hand. Rub the object inside to feel the texture. Then replace the sock in the basket.
3. Place the basket in front of him and allow ample time for exploration.

Note: Make sure the objects in the socks are safe to mouth and explore.

Row, Row Tones

When you sing, your baby is learning tones that are relative to one another within a song. Emphasizing these tones outside of the song itself can help develop concentration.

1. While sitting in front of your baby, sing the song "Row, Row, Row Your Boat."
2. Next, hum the song in its entirety.
3. Now you're going to hum single tones. For example, very slowly and in order, hum the tones that go with these words: "row," "boat," "stream," "merrily," "life," "but," and "dream."
4. Play around with these tones, humming them in different patterns while your baby listens. For example, you might hum the tones for row-boat-row-boat. Or you might hum the tones for the pattern row-boat-stream-boat-row.

> **Row**, row, row your **boat**
> Gently down the **stream**
> **Merrily**, merrily, merrily, merrily
> **Life** is but a **dream**

Note: The first time you try this activity, it may feel challenging, but the more you practice, the more intuitive it will get. You can use the same technique for any short, easy song with a simple musical pattern. Try it with "Mary Had a Little Lamb" or "Hot Cross Buns."

Language and Mental Development

Receptive language develops far sooner than expressive language, which means your baby knows more than she can say. You and your baby can have regular conversations now, both verbal and nonverbal. Gestures and sign language, such as "all done" and "happy," continue to aid your baby in communicating desires and emotions. She may be pointing at things to prompt you for new vocabulary words. She also continues stringing together consonants and vowels, babbling both to people and out loud just for practice.

Your baby may also be saying a first word or two, heavily modified from adult speech. The word "ball" may sound like "bah" and the word "milk" may come out like "mi." It's fun to anticipate what your baby's first word will be, but it might take you by surprise.

Milestones

- **Understands a wide variety of words:** While not talking much, your baby comprehends a considerable amount of your spoken language. Demonstrating a true understanding of familiar words and phrases is also easier for him now that he can point, giggle, and gesture to objects or people.
- **Converses eagerly back and forth:** It may still sound like gibberish to you, but when your baby babbles on and then pauses, looks at you intently, and then continues babbling, there are sure to be complex ideas and thoughts going through his head. By participating in his "conversation," you are acknowledging his efforts to communicate. It's okay if you don't have any idea what he's saying. Talk back, and enjoy interacting.
- **Verbalizes a few words:** It's about this age that some babies are able to focus deeply enough to cut out the babbling and utter a distinct word or two like "mama" or "dada." If your baby isn't talking yet, no need to worry. Most babies will say a first word sometime between 9 and 14 months.
- **Understands brief requests for action:** If you ask your baby to do a specific action, such as give you a toy, share a bite of cracker, or point to an object, he may begin honoring these little requests. Remember that anything you ask him to do must be one extremely short step.

- **Plays finger-pointing vocabulary games:** Your baby is always looking for ways to increase her vocabulary and enjoys looking at pictures or objects and hearing you say the words. Games like this can be played anywhere and at any time.

Games and Activities

Five Little Fish

This fun fingerplay is great for teaching action words.

1. Tell your baby you would like to play a game with his fingers.
2. Start by holding one of your baby's hands gently in your palm with one hand. During the first line, rub your baby's palm in a circle.
3. Then use your index finger and thumb to wiggle each finger in succession while you say this rhyme in a high-pitched, exaggerated tone of voice.
4. Begin with the thumb and end with the pinkie finger.
5. Finish this game with a pretend dive into your baby's belly.

Five little fish in a little fish bowl	(rub baby's palm)
One fish flips	(wiggle thumb)
One fish dips	(wiggle index finger)
One fish wiggles	(wiggle middle finger)
One fish jiggles	(wiggle ring finger)
And the last little fishy does	
a great big dive!	(wiggle pinkie finger and dive down toward baby's belly)

Where Is the Animal?

Toy animals offer many opportunities for vocabulary building. For this game, you need two toy animals and one opaque or transparent container that can cover one toy at a time.

1. Place two toy animals in front of your baby. Name each one and describe its characteristics. For example, "This is a cow. It says moo. Cows are big animals. They live on a farm and like to eat grass."
2. Put the toy animal back down again and ask her to point to it. For example, ask "Where is the cow? Can you find the cow?"
3. Repeat this experience with the other toy animal.

4. Now hide one of the animals inside the container and ask her where that animal is. Allow her to lift up the container and find it while you happily say its name again. For example, "You found the cow! The cow was hiding under there!"
5. Repeat this experience with the other toy animal.
6. Now let her sit and explore the three items in any way she likes.

What I Wear

Giving your baby choices while getting dressed conveys respect, enhances vocabulary, and prepares your baby for future independence. You can model making similar choices when you get dressed. In time, he will emulate you when getting dressed himself.

1. When dressing your baby, hold up the item you intend to put on first and say the name of the item. For example, you might say, "First, we're going to put on a shirt."
2. If there is an acceptable choice, ask him if he would like to wear one item or another. For example, you might say, "Would you like to wear the red shirt or the blue shirt?" If he reaches for one of the shirts, tell him that this seems like a nice choice.

3. Allow a few seconds for him to feel the item of clothing, and then describe the process as you put it on. For example, you might say, "Now I'm going to put your head through the top. Here is an opening for one arm. I'll help you get your arm through . . ."
4. Repeat this process for the remaining items of clothing.

YOUR BAREFOOT BABY

Your baby might be pulling up and getting ready to walk, but don't be too quick to cover those tootsies. There are immense advantages to giving your child as much barefoot time as possible. You may notice that your baby's foot is flat on the bottom. Over time, as your little one learns to walk, skip, hop, and jump without shoes, the muscles and ligaments will strengthen, creating a strong, natural arch. Walking barefoot also helps develop balance and good posture.

Of course, if it's too cold or hot outside, or just not a safe place to explore in bare feet, give those little feet some protection. Choose soft-soled shoes that are flexible and mold to the shape of your baby's foot, allowing the toes to spread rather than being confined into a stiff shape.

Social-Emotional Skills

Being a copycat is a compliment at this playful age. Your baby may be absolutely delighting in your willingness to be imitated and be a mimic. For example, if you regularly use a sponge to wipe your baby's table, you may see your baby imitating this motion. If you make a funny coughing sound, your baby might do the same. And the reverse is just as fun: When you copy their movements, you are showing that you care.

Separation anxiety continues as part of your baby's temporary personality. This clinginess may cause you to feel anxious yourself, but a strong attachment to a parent is healthy. Sometimes, it may be difficult for you to feel so needed all the time. If you need to take a break, tell your baby you are leaving instead of slipping away unnoticed (see "Saying Bye-Bye" on page 79).

Milestones

- **Closely observes your behavior toward others:** From the kind, respectful words you use to the way you wait patiently for your turn, your baby is very much aware of the many social gestures that indicate respect for other people.
- **Imitates the activities of others:** If you put glasses on, you may be surprised to see your baby touching the sides of his face with the same motion. Imitating your purposeful movements is one way your baby is learning to interpret your intentions. Many babies can start to participate in household chores and imitate the ways that older children play.
- **Watches to make sure you remain close by:** Even if your baby is happily playing nearby, you may notice quick little glances in your direction to see if you are still present. If you seem to disappear without warning, she may look worried or crawl to the place where you were last observed.
- **Initiates the "copycat" game:** Babies like it when you copy them. This interaction often begins when your baby makes a sound or gesture to get your attention. When you mimic the sound or action, she will continue the game, looking back to see if you are going to copy her again.
- **Gives and takes objects:** Often, 9- and 10-month-olds reach out to hand you an object. When you take it, you can say thank you and then pass it back. Most babies enjoy practicing giving and receiving.

Games and Activities

Follow Me

Embrace your inner mischief-making side and get down on the floor to crawl around with your baby.

1. When your baby is active and playfully crawling around, get on your own hands and knees and crawl toward a doorway.
2. Peek around the doorway to see if she is following you. If not, call her name to encourage her to come.
3. Keep crawling for a few minutes if your baby is crawling after you, and then let yourself be "caught" by her.
4. Now reverse the game and crawl after her. Wait until you're sure she wants to get "caught" before catching her up in your arms for a hug and kiss.

First Me, Then You

This copycat game will be one you can repeat over and over for the next year. Start now with a very simple version.

1. Sit down in front of your baby with two of the exact same objects. For example, two toy rattles or two cups.
2. Pick up one of the objects and do something unexpected with it like hold it up in the air, pat the floor with it or turn it upside down.
3. Watch to see if he copies your actions. If not, that is perfectly okay. Reverse the game at this point and copy his actions instead.
4. At some point in time, after you have played this game a few times, he may think it's pretty funny. Enjoy being silly together.

We Can Brush Our Hair

While your baby may not have much hair yet to brush, giving her a soft hairbrush will set the stage for self-care. You might incorporate this activity into your own morning routine.

1. Sit down in front of your baby with your hairbrush in your hand. Begin to brush your hair very slowly and silently. Watch to see if she is paying attention.
2. Now give her a small, soft hairbrush to hold. Allow her to examine and explore it.
3. Continue brushing your hair slowly and deliberately. She may imitate you and make similar motions.
4. Repeat this activity so that your baby understands that this activity is a regular habit.

Notes

Words my baby responded to this month include . . .

_____

_____

_____

_____

_____

_____

_____

Some messy play my baby enjoyed this month was . . .

_____

_____

_____

_____

_____

_____

_____

MONTH
11

Your Baby This Month

Your baby is probably looking much more like an active, busy toddler than a baby. Your life together is changing every day as you approach the end of the first year.

It may still be a while yet before your baby is walking independently, but by now most babies know how to get around when they are motivated to get to a toy. If you aren't seeing this kind of mobility yet, keep placing interesting objects a few feet or even a few yards away from your baby's reach, and don't stress. Some babies are just happy to hang out wherever they are until inspiration hits.

The world is full of fascinating objects to manipulate, foods to try, and people to meet, even if your little one feels shy around strangers. The close and trusting relationship you have worked to build with him since the moment of birth is a gift for your future together. As he grows into more of an independent being and begins to slowly separate from you psychologically and physically, that secure bond will be even more appreciated.

Challenges This Month

- **Naps:** Babies who take the typical morning and afternoon naps may soon drop one. The morning nap is typically dropped first, but not always. Some babies will attempt to stop napping altogether because playtime has become such fun. While you can't make a baby fall asleep or stay asleep, the right environment and a consistent routine can be effective encouragement. Even if she stays awake during naptime, having regular quiet time can give her a chance to recharge.
- **Listening:** The world is so captivating that getting your baby's attention might require more effort on your part. To make sure your baby is listening to you, get close, look into her eyes, and maintain eye contact. Speaking in a soft voice up close is also often more effective than yelling from afar.
- **Tipping objects over:** Your home may feel like a disaster zone by the time your baby is done with playtime. For the next year, your little one will find cause and effect absolutely delightful, but you might find it tiresome as you pick up the toys she drops and scatters on purpose. Keep the selection of toys to a manageable level, and use open storage—for example, small baskets or a low shelf that your baby can access. If you keep calmly modeling how to put items back where they belong and make the process simple, your toddler will start to emulate this behavior in the next several months.

Highlights This Month

- **Playing ball:** Sometime soon, if not already, your baby will be capable of rolling a ball back and forth with you. Sit a few feet away with your legs spread apart and roll the ball to your baby. She may choose to catch and roll the ball back to you or explore its properties on her own. Either decision is fine and will lead to learning opportunities for your little one.
- **Making choices:** Your baby is able to show you more clearly which of two items is preferred, so offering her simple choices gently introduces her to a more independent lifestyle. When offering choices, make sure that both options are safe and acceptable.
- **Receptive language:** Listening to your adult speech is critical. Using short, clear sentences when communicating with your baby is fine and aids his comprehension, but try not to use much baby talk to change the words and phrases themselves. Your baby is listening very intently for the correct pronunciation to imitate.

Motor Skills

Most babies are pulling up fairly well and practicing some standing and cruising. When your baby starts moving around upright, his gait likely starts with an adorable waddling, back-and-forth rocking motion. This extra momentum is usually needed to propel his body forward effectively. These initial attempts become smoother and smoother with practice.

You may enjoy holding your little one's hand, although at this stage the desire for actual hand-holding will not be mutual. Instead, think of yourself as offering another stable place for support, both moral and physical. Let your baby take the lead here and do all of the balancing work. Resist the urge to offer too much assistance. Keep your arms steady and your grip loose. You want to bolster confidence, but you don't want him to throw caution to the wind. That bit of caution and the knowledge of his current capabilities will come in handy when encountering a flight of stairs.

Milestones

- **Sits from a standing position:** Most babies are getting pretty good at standing by this month, and some are even sitting down from standing without losing balance or toppling backward. This new ability bolsters confidence while cruising because your baby knows that any time he feels unstable, sitting down is always an option.
- **Holds your hand to stand:** If you hold out a hand, your baby may just take it and pull up to a stand. Knowing that you are close by for emotional and physical assistance can make all the difference in his desire to keep practicing pulling up and holding the position.
- **Stands alone for brief periods:** Some babies are getting so comfortable pulling up and standing that they are successful in letting go for a few seconds. A few even take a few steps before sitting back down.
- **Cruises around the furniture:** Furniture may have become a gym for gross motor development. Many babies practice cruising from one piece of furniture to the next, pausing to crawl to the next place to pull up.
- **Dumps and fills containers:** While fine motor skills are still a big focus for this month, you might notice your baby squealing with glee while dumping out objects onto the floor. Support this developmental need by providing open containers, such as baskets or bowls, that your baby can fill with interesting objects. He can then dump everything out and start again.

Games and Activities

Beanbag Bucket

Develop your child's motor skills using objects that also offer a tactile experience.

1. Fill a basket or bucket, about a foot tall, with 5 to 10 beanbags.
2. Call to your baby and then have her watch you slowly carry the bucket and place it on the floor near her.
3. Show her how to tip the bucket over, dumping all of the beanbags out onto the floor. Place each back in one at a time.
4. Allow her to explore all of these items freely with you watching her. When she's done, store the beanbags out of reach.

Note: To make beanbags, cut sturdy fabric into five-inch squares and use dried beans for filling. Sew the edges securely and reinforce the seams to prevent rips that would allow beans, which are a choking hazard, to come out. Never leave your child unattended with beanbags, and always check them for rips before playing.

Ring around the Baby

Try this gentle, toned-down variation of an old classic to encourage your baby to sit down from a standing position.

1. Stoop down and hold your hands out for him to firmly grasp. Allow him to pull himself up to a standing position.
2. Sing this rhyme, using your child's name in the third line, and sit down together at the end.

   Standing with my baby
   Pockets full of daisies
   I love you, [your child's name]
   We both sit down!

Note: Never pull your baby down into a sitting position. Rather, keep your hands level to provide enough support and sit down gently, allowing him to keep standing if desired.

Cruisin' Around

Your baby will want to cruise on over when she sees what's in your lap.

1. If your baby is pulling up on furniture and beginning to cruise, sit down on the far end of a couch with a hidden toy in your lap, loosely wrapped in cloth.
2. Tell her you have something for her to see. Hold up the object (which is hidden inside the cloth).
3. When she cruises over and reaches you, offer the hidden object and let her unwrap it to discover what is inside.

Sensory Development

Your baby's basic senses are all very well developed by now. Your baby's vision is just about as good as your own when it comes to observing shapes from near and far, inspecting tiny objects, and tracking moving objects. He is no longer practicing the development of these skills but is actually using them in daily life to learn more about the world—just like you do.

Interacting may begin to feel more educational in nature. Gone are the days when your baby could just sit and enjoy a toy for its simple properties. You are welcoming in a new era of sensory learning: one where exploring the effects one's own body can have on an object is much more interesting than just feeling or tasting. Your baby is keen to hear you explain, observe your actions, and then give them a try.

Milestones

- **Has fully developed vision:** By this month, your baby sees the world much like an adult. Quickly moving objects can be tracked rapidly, even from a distance. If you can see it, she can, too.
- **Listens and looks at the same time:** Your baby has been practicing both of these skills separately for the past 10 months, but now they are working in sync. This means that even though she is looking at a toy, those little ears still perk up, tuned in to your voice.
- **Tries to alter flimsy objects:** Your baby may be testing out the powers of stronger fingers and thumbs, poking, pinching, and pulling at objects to explore them. The sound and sight of paper ripping after being pinched or poked might make her giggle or gasp.

Games and Activities

Catch a Bubble

Flying bubbles capture your baby's attention. For this activity, you'll need child-safe bubble solution and a bubble wand.

1. Go outside together and sit on the ground.
2. Show her the solution and the wand.
3. Stand up briefly to blow a few bubbles up in the air. Then sit back down right away.
4. Point to the bubbles floating and follow them with your eyes while saying the bubble poem.

Bubble, bubble in the air,
Watch it fly and float up there.
Bubble, bubble, coming down,
Watch it drifting to the ground.

Note: Never leave your baby unattended with liquids, including bubble solution.

Paint Smudging

Let's put those poking, prodding fingers to good use! You'll need several colors of child-safe paint with a goopy texture for this color experiment. Consider using the primary colors: yellow, red, and blue.

1. Place several dollops of different color paint on a blank painting canvas.
2. Wrap the canvas in plastic wrap and set it down in front of your baby.
3. Show him how to poke, smear, smudge, and rub the plastic so that the paint begins to blend together in places.
4. Unwrap the canvas and allow his artwork to dry. Dispose of the plastic wrap and store the paint away.

Note: Never leave your child unattended with the plastic wrap or paints.

Tearing Paper

The sound of ripping paper might just be fascinating.

1. Gather a stack of easy-to-tear paper, like tissue paper or newspaper.
2. Sit down with your baby. Hold a piece of paper in your hands, tear it a few inches, and show her how the paper can be torn all the way in half.
3. Tear another piece of paper a few inches, have your baby hold one side, and finish tearing paper between the two of you.
4. If she is successful at tearing the paper with you, give her the paper to tear all on her own.

Note: Never leave your baby unattended with paper, which can be a choking hazard.

Language and Mental Development

Every time you have a conversation with your little one, the speech patterns you use become clearer and more distinct in his mind. You won't be able to see this cognitive development, but your child is understanding a lot more words and phrases. Reading books with realistic-looking photos or looking at pictures of common objects and animals from a set of cards is a great way to both build vocabulary and, depending on how he responds, start to get a sense of what he already knows.

The absolute best thing you can do to nurture your child's language skills is to have natural conversations in the context of the current activity or environment. The connection of words to meaning is then reinforced when you look at pictures of familiar objects and animals and have extended conversations about them. You can remind him of the last time he encountered the object in a picture in real life or talk about where you would find it—for example, a frog in a pond—and give some background about it.

Note: You may come across products that claim to boost your baby's vocabulary or even offer a method to teach your baby to read. Do they work? Well, a baby's brain is capable of amazing accomplishments, but using electronic toys, flash cards with words, or other memorization techniques for quick recall of words is not the best use of your baby's time.

Milestones

- **Uses gestures, signs, and hand motions with purpose:** The gestures your baby has been making are more automatic and naturally expressive. Nods give assent. Hands wave bye-bye when leaving. If you have been teaching your baby sign language, you might find that she responds more quickly and is more expressive with these motions than with words.
- **Increased receptive language vocabulary:** Little ears around you are always listening in on your conversations. When you speak to another person, you might not be able to keep the topic a secret anymore. For example, if you talk about the park, your baby may wonder if you will be going there. If you mention your shoes, your baby might go find them. When you're talking to her, ask a lot of simple questions and wait to see if she responds with a gesture or vocalization before answering it yourself.

- **Increased expressive language:** By the end of this year, about half of all babies are able to say a word or two. Others remain quiet into the second year, but most have met this milestone by 14 months. If your baby is already talking, the number of spoken words may be increasing already, although not as quickly as her receptive vocabulary.
- **Practices using known words in context:** Most babies spend a good amount of time practicing the words they know, and it's good for them to hear these words repeated back to them in context. Emphasizing these words in your own speech demonstrates how they are used to convey special meanings.

Games and Activities

Picture Hunt

Reading together provides countless opportunities for vocabulary development.

1. Sit down with your baby in front of a basket that contains a handful of board books.
2. Allow him to choose which book to read.
3. As you turn the pages in the book, ask him to point to various pictures. For example, you might say, "Where is the cat? Can you point to the cat?"
4. If he points to the correct object, there is no need to praise. Instead, offer a simple confirmation. For example, "You found the cat."
5. If he points to a different picture, there is no need to criticize or correct. Simply comment on what he is pointing at instead. For example, "You see a dog. I see the dog, too. Now let's find the cat."
6. If your baby does not seem interested in pointing, continue to model this activity yourself by pointing to various objects as you read.

Bring Me

Mission: Find and bring back a specified object.

1. Strategically place a few familiar objects or toys around the room.
2. Sit in the middle of the room with your baby and point out one of the objects that would be fun to play with together. For example, you might say, "I see a ball over there."
3. Suggest to her that she be the one to go get the object. For example, you might say, "Would you bring me the ball so we can play with it?"

A Simple Story

Hone in on your baby's receptive language skills by telling a very simple, reality-based story.

1. Start by choosing a topic for your story. Make sure it is something that is relevant to your baby's range of real-life experiences. For example, you might tell the story of your latest trip to the grocery store or park.
2. Capture his attention by looking intently into his eyes.
3. Using the story script below as a guideline, tell your story in a dramatic tone of voice with varied inflection. Embellish your sentences with descriptive words, such as "silky," "gigantic," "noisy," or "brave."
4. Pause now and then to ask him a question. For example, you might say, "Do you remember when we smelled the oranges?"
5. If it is helpful, you may use the sentence prompts below for storytelling inspiration.

The beginning: One day . . . And then . . .
The middle: But . . . So . . .
The ending: Finally . . .

BEING IN NATURE

Simply being in nature has an impact on the mental and emotional well-being of humans, and babies are no exception to the rule. Many parents find that their babies, when in a grouchy or overly excitable mood at home, calm down and become peaceful when taken outdoors for a walk.

Learning to care for and appreciate nature begins in early childhood. As long as you use plenty of sun protection and appropriate clothing for the weather, you can spend quite a bit of time outdoors with your baby exploring bits of nature, singing songs, and using the senses to learn more about the natural world.

Social-Emotional Skills

Independence is not found through a peaceful acceptance of new skills but through challenging the status quo. As a result, your baby may resist your normal routines, insist on doing things a certain way, or express distress until a lost object has been found. It is these little struggles that lead to the confident adult you hope your child will become. No matter how frustrating or unreasonable it can be, take comfort in the knowledge that she is simply learning how to assert her wants and needs, a valuable life skill for the future.

It may seem odd that at the same time your baby is practicing assertiveness, a more cautious, hesitant, and even irrationally fearful side of her personality is also emerging. When you don't sense any danger yourself, it can be easy to dismiss her fears. When she acts scared by a person, object, or situation, try to remain calm and comforting, but don't overreact or force her to have a close encounter with the source of these troubled emotions. These anxieties typically subside on their own.

Milestones

- **Recognizes self in mirror:** It must be a strangely wonderous feeling for your baby to finally recognize his own face in a reflected surface. Along with this realization may come a sudden renewed interest in mirror play—touching body parts and making gestures that can be seen in the mirror and felt in real life at the same time.
- **Raises arms to be picked up:** By now your baby is likely to tell you exactly when he wants to be picked up.
- **Exhibits more caution:** New experiences can be intimidating. Your baby has had enough experiences to know that not everything is pleasant. Trying new foods or exploring new places may be met with hesitation.
- **Consistent, irrational fears:** Aside from the separation anxiety, your baby may suddenly become fearful of familiar sounds and objects. Common fears still include the vacuum cleaner, the toilet flushing, and barking dogs. For most children, this is temporary and will resolve on its own in time.
- **Becomes more assertive:** This new side of your baby's personality may take you by surprise. For most of the first year, babies are tuned in entirely to the present moment, depending on you to make decisions. However, now many babies decide they want to have a say in things. Whether he likes or dislikes an activity becomes much clearer, and expect your baby to be a lot more determined to get what he wants.

Games and Activities

The Sky Is on the Ground

For a twist on mirror reflection play, bring an unbreakable mirror with you to the park.

1. Set the mirror on the ground a few feet in front of your baby. Make sure that the sun is not directly overhead and cannot be viewed through the mirror.
2. Encourage her to go take a peek inside to see who is looking back.

Up, Up and Away

Encourage your baby to raise both arms up toward you to be picked up by practicing the gesture in the form of this game.

1. While your baby is seated in front of you, raise both of your arms in the air and say, "Do you want to come up?"
2. If he seems agreeable or mimics your movements, say, "Up, up, and away" as you gently lift him into the air and take a few steps backward.
3. Tell him you are coming back down and gently return him to the start position.

Not Scary

Help your baby overcome new fears by talking about the topic.

1. Bring your baby to a safe distance where the object or a picture of the object can be viewed without fear.
2. Tell her some facts about the object. For example, you might say, "The vacuum cleaner is noisy, but I like it. It's not scary. It sucks up the dirt and dust so that we can keep our carpet clean."
3. Make sure your conversation stays light, positive, and without pressure.

Notes

This month, my baby is more cautious of . . .

This month, my baby understands these words/phrases:

MONTH

12

Your Baby This Month

Your little baby will soon be one year old. Whether he's still crawling for a few months or already toddling about, life with your little one will be different next year. The two of you are both well prepared now for all of the changes in development coming your way. Every time you sat down to rock, feed, sing a lullaby, or whisper words of love, you were calming the nervous system, setting the stage for a secure attachment that has a lifetime of emotional benefits. Your baby is now learning to feel like a separate person with original thoughts, physical independence, and more complex goals.

Your baby is taking on more complicated activities, which require more concentration. When he makes what look to you like mistakes, resist any temptation to jump in and show him what you see as the correct or more efficient way to do things. Hold yourself back from helping too soon and too often, and he will learn a lesson much greater than any separate skill: perseverance. Trust in your child, and enter the next year with confidence.

Challenges This Month

- **Spills and splashes:** When you think about it, water really is a strange substance to explore. It can take on the shape of any container, but when poured out, it flattens instantly, forming a puddle that can shine back your reflection. It's no wonder babies delight in spilling liquid and splashing in it. Whenever you know your baby will be around a source of water, embrace the fun within reasonable limits and be ready with a change of clothing. (Never leave your baby unattended near water.)
- **Birthday party preparation:** Your baby will not understand the purpose of a birthday party celebrating his first year. Consider how comfortable he is around other people when you plan a party. If he gets nervous around large groups, a smaller, calmer party in a familiar location could be more baby-friendly.

Highlights This Month

- **Playground adventures:** Your little mountaineer may be excited to climb and explore new heights. Playgrounds can be full of older children who aren't watching out for your baby, so you'll need to supervise extra closely while you enjoy exploring these new challenges together.
- **Affection:** Your baby has more self-awareness and will let you know how appreciated you are in many ways, even if they are still primarily nonverbal. When she gives you brief hugs and wet kisses, reaches up to be in your arms, and cries when you're out of sight, you know that you are well loved.

Motor Skills

Toward the end of the first year, your baby is itching to learn to walk. Some babies take this leap as early as nine months, and some babies take until several months after their first birthdays. Either way, your job is mostly to have patience, giving your baby the time and physical freedom to learn this new, life-changing skill. If she still isn't walking by about 18 months, bring it up with your baby's doctor. Otherwise, enjoy those cute crawling or shuffling movements while they last and trust that your baby is developing at the perfect pace.

Milestones

- **Stoops from a standing position:** By the end of this month, about a quarter of babies will be practicing bending over and standing straight back up again. When a toy is dropped onto the floor, it will be much easier for your baby to bend over to pick it up. You may even see your baby do this over and over again on purpose to practice this skill.

- **Goes up and down stairs:** Most of the time babies learn how to walk or crawl up stairs first before sliding back down feet first on their bellies. Either way, until your baby has the movement down securely, make sure you are right behind her to catch any unexpected tumbles. Most babies learn to go up and down somewhere between 12 and 15 months.

- **Turns pages of a book:** The pincer grasp is being put to very good use when reading a book together. If you lift and hold a page out steady, your baby may be able to pinch the corner and turn it over so that you can read the next one. This is a preliteracy skill.

- **May take first steps:** No one can tell you exactly when your baby will take those first steps, but when he does, a real toddler isn't too far off. To encourage this milestone, allow lots of time for your baby to practice cruising and balancing while standing still. It can take time for your baby to learn to lift each leg, one at a time, in a coordinated rhythmic motion. It will also take a good bit of bravery to leave support behind. If your baby isn't expressing interest in walking yet, patience will be your friend. Some babies won't take their first real steps for another five months or so.

- **Transfers objects:** Your baby is getting more adept at picking up objects from one spot and transferring them to another spot. At first, your baby will likely be working with only one container, such as taking balls in and out of a basket. When this skill is well developed, your baby will work with two containers at a time, transferring objects back and forth between them. You might even see your baby holding two objects in one hand while working with the other hand.

Games and Activities

Playing Detective

Digging in a bag or purse for keys or other objects can be awfully exciting. This would be a great activity to bring with you on a road trip.

1. Fill an extra handbag with baby-friendly objects, such as small toys, placing one object inside each pocket of the bag. (Choose a handbag that has no parts that could detach and be choking hazards.)
2. Present the bag to your baby, open up the top, peer inside, and say, "I wonder what's in there."
3. Allow her to reach in, dump out, and generally explore the bag.
4. When finished, model replacing the items inside, letting her help if she wants to.

Nesting Cup Exploration

Nesting cups are versatile toys, offering lots of opportunities to practice fine motor skills, such as stacking.

1. Sit next to your baby and place two nesting cups in front of him.
2. Demonstrate how the cups slide together to form one and then slide apart again to make two.
3. If he is proficient with the first two, offer more cups at one time.
4. For a variation, add a set of objects (one for each cup) and allow him to explore putting the objects inside of the cups and taking them back out again.

Pushing to Walk

If your baby is pulling up and cruising, he may like a toy that he can push to practice the motion of walking while still having his balance supported.

1. Select a commercially available push toy or a sturdy piece of furniture that can slide or roll on a smooth surface (such as a stool with felt on the bottom of the legs). Make sure it won't easily tip and does not roll too quickly.
2. Show your baby how to hold the pushing toy with two hands and walk forward.
3. While he holds on for the first time, provide a hand on his back to show that he is safe and protected while learning how to use this new toy.

Note: Do not use a "baby walker" where your baby sits inside a seat while pushing herself around with her legs. What you are looking for instead is an object that your baby can push and walk with, doing all the hard work by herself.

Sensory Development

With almost a year of sensory experiences to draw from, your baby is busy making deeper, more focused connections with both objects and the surrounding environment. The increase in focus and attention will slightly alter your habits and routines. You may, for example, read together for longer and longer periods of time. During playtime, you will find more moments when your baby needs you to take a step back and keep mum, not interrupting his focus unless absolutely necessary. Your baby instinctively knows how long to explore a material and when it's time to move on. Trust in this natural ability.

However, you can help your baby make more intense sensory discoveries by offering more experiences that isolate the senses. Clearing the play area of noisy or visual distractions is one easy way to do this in the home. Outdoors, be on the lookout for quiet, smaller spaces to explore, like the perfect puddle to splash in together or a soft patch of grass just right for bare feet.

Milestones

- **Increased focus and attention:** Your baby can tune out extraneous noises and background activity more easily, allowing an increase in focus on a single task for longer periods of time. You are more likely to be able to read a book with your baby from start to finish now. Eating and playing become more serious business toward the end of this month.
- **Thrives on human touch:** Independence is blooming, but your baby still needs lots of physical contact with you. He might like you to carry him in a sling or soft-structured carrier so he can have regular close contact with you during daily activities or while being transported from one area to another. You might also notice that he enjoys a gentle backrub or a caress on the top of his head.
- **Nurses for comfort:** If you are breastfeeding, you may find that your baby regularly asks to return to the breast specifically for comfort. Non-breastfeeding parents may find their babies seeking a similar downtime by curling up in a lap for extended cuddles or rocking.

- **Returns hugs and kisses:** The feeling of being hugged or kissed is a pleasurable sensory experience for most children, and by now your baby may equally enjoy the sensation of kissing and hugging back.
- **Seeks isolated sensory experiences:** Complex sensory experiences that engage several senses at once are an inescapable part of life. To avoid being overwhelmed and to learn more about the world, your baby is starting to concentrate more deeply on one sensation at a time.

Games and Activities

Footprint Painting

Capture those tiny footprints on a piece of paper that doubles as a sensory play surface.

1. To prepare for this activity, saturate a rectangular, medium-size sponge in nontoxic acrylic paint and place it inside a container. Spread a large piece of paper outside, in the bathtub, or in an area where you're okay with the possibility of a little paint getting on the floor.
2. While your baby is sitting in your lap, press one foot into the sponge for a sensory experience isolated to only one part of his body.
3. Help him stand up, and hold his hands as he walks on the paper.
4. If he wants to repeat the experience right away, switch feet and walk-paint with the other foot.

Tip: Have a bowl of warm water and a washcloth ready to wipe his feet when the painting experience is finished. (Never leave your baby unattended near water.)

Feel the Wind

The feeling of moving air on one's skin is a sensation your baby might enjoy.

1. Sit with your baby on the floor and hold out one of your own arms. Gently blow on it.
2. Say, "I feel the air on my skin." Ask her if she would like to feel it, too.
3. If she consents by looking inquisitive, blow gently on her arm, too.
4. Repeat the experience with different body parts.

Pouring Water

Pair a tiny unbreakable cup with a tiny unbreakable creamer pitcher to give your baby more freedom to explore the properties of water.

1. Fill the tiny pitcher with a couple of ounces of water. Just a little bit will do. Have a cloth ready to dry spills.
2. Place the pitcher next to the empty cup. Demonstrate very slowly and carefully how to pour a little bit of water from the pitcher into the cup and take a sip.
3. Allow your baby to take the pitcher and explore. He may spill the water on purpose in order to play in it, and this is part of the experience. Offer him the cloth and help him wipe up any spills.
4. Repeat this activity often to allow your baby to practice the skill of pouring while exploring the properties of water.

Language and Mental Development

Remember those first little coos? Those tentative exploratory vowel sounds marked the beginning of a year of hard work imitating sounds and learning which ones were relevant to your baby's own native tongue. Communicating with your baby is so different now. You no longer need to wonder what your baby likes or doesn't like. There are many expressive ways she can tell you. Her brain is also capable of more complex thinking, anticipating familiar activities and figuring out how new toys work with aplomb.

If you are a bilingual or multilingual family, your baby may have been well exposed to more than one language. Many bilingual babies say their first words just slightly on the later side of the typical age range, and some words and phrases may be a little mixed up at first, but this is very normal and to be expected. Being able to speak two or more languages comes with vast advantages, and during infancy is the best possible time to introduce them.

Milestones

- **Demonstrates problem-solving skills:** Your baby likely already knows from prior experiences that she can roll balls, lift lids, push buttons, and turn knobs. By the end of this month, she will be able to gauge the likelihood that a new object can be manipulated in a certain way. Activities that require more than one step are also a point of interest. Throughout the following year, you will see her continue to approach increasingly complex, multistep tasks with more determination and purpose.
- **Responds to one-step commands:** To assess receptive language skills, you might ask your baby to bring you an object, such as a favorite toy or an item of clothing. The ability to follow multistep verbal directions is probably about a year away, so for now, keep your instructions short, simple, and very direct.
- **Responds to simple questions:** All that practice pointing, nodding, and using other hand signs or body gestures has now allowed your baby to communicate quite a bit of information. If you ask "Would you like a drink of water?" you might see a slight nod or an exaggerated one, but the way in which she responds will be more consistent.

- **Makes simple choices:** When given a choice between two items, your baby is now capable of making a conscious decision and is also able to tell you which one is preferred. Start practicing this skill with only two items. For example, "Would you like to drink out of the blue cup or the green cup?" As she becomes more decisive about making choices, you can offer more options. If she seems overwhelmed, consider paring back the number of choices again.

Games and Activities

What's Cooking?

Babies love to be involved in real-life experiences like hanging out with you in the kitchen while you cook.

1. Allow your baby to participate in different stages of the cooking process.
2. Begin by hunting for ingredients together. Ask your baby to point to the food you are looking for. For example, say, "Can you find a potato? We keep them in this drawer. Do you see one for our soup?"
3. Describe what you are going to do with the ingredients. For example, "I am going to scrub the potato first to get it clean. Would you like to come with me to the sink?"
4. Offer choices to your baby that will engage the senses while you work. "Would you like to feel the potato or the carrot?"
5. While you're cooking, talk about the process and involve your baby by naming ingredients.

Note: Safety is your number one priority in the kitchen. While using a sharp knife, hot stove, or other kitchen appliances, be sure that your baby is safely far enough away. This might be a good time to offer a kitchen treasure basket on the floor (see page 100).

Modeling Choices

A very low shelf with cubbies, each holding just a few toys, allows your baby to make clear choices about what to play with, but your baby will need modeling and encouragement.

1. Sit with your baby in front of the shelf.
2. Announce that you will choose a toy to play with. For example, say, "I'm going to choose something from this shelf. I wonder what I'd like to play with now."
3. Pick up a toy and say, "I choose this." Manipulate the toy briefly in front of her.

4. Now say, "I'm finished playing with this one," and put the toy back on the shelf exactly where you found it.
5. Ask your baby if she would like to choose.

Note: All shelves your baby can access should be anchored securely to the wall.

Preposition Playtime

A toy and a box—so much learning can happen with this very simple setup.

1. Show your baby a small toy, such as a plush or plastic animal. Describe it and let him touch it.
2. Now set it next to a container or box big enough to hold the toy.
3. Give him very brief, one-step commands or ask simple questions about what to do with the toy. For example, you might say playfully, "Where can we put the doggie? Can he go inside the box? He can. Now let's take him out of the box."
4. During this game, try using preposition words and phrases such as "inside," "outside," "around," "behind," "in front of," "next to," "on top of," and "under."

Social-Emotional Skills

Increasing signs of independence will offer both warm, happy times to celebrate, such as when your baby learns to pet a kitty ever so gently, and stormy times to weather, such as when your baby refuses to nap for fear of missing out on something and then cries from sheer exhaustion.

It's possible that you may even begin to encounter the first signs of the classic toddler tantrum. Tantrums at this age are typically very mild and easily handled, so don't fear this stage; face it head-on. A tantrum is simply your child's expression of frustration, sadness, or anger. At this stage, the best way to handle an outburst of unhappiness is to stay calm and soothe your little one. Whether it's cuddling, rocking, nursing, or just sitting patiently nearby, you will be letting your baby know that you care. Providing a change of scenery, removing the offending object, or offering a new activity may also be helpful after you have allowed your baby to express these big emotions.

Milestones

- **Demands independence:** The drive toward independence, even when not yet capable, is ramping up toward the end of the first year. Your baby might be enthusiastically self-feeding solids, getting more proficient using a cup, and taking off a diaper or resisting diaper changes. Babies this age are also impulsive explorers and may be trying to climb over barriers to get into places that are off-limits.
- **Exhibits cooperative behavior:** Arms go up; shirt goes on. Legs stick out; pants slide up. If you have noticed more participation recently when dressing your baby, this is a sign that your baby is aware of the activity and is trying to be helpful. Eventually, your little one will learn to do these tasks independently, but for now, the two of you may become more of a team.
- **Becomes frustrated when hungry or tired:** As much as you try to anticipate your baby's basic needs for food and sleep, the truth is that the world is soooo exciting and your baby soooo busy that those needs can sneak up on both of you. A new very characteristic temperament of this age when your baby is hungry or tired is grumpiness or extra frustration. Be on the lookout and bring some snacks with you when you go out.

- **May throw tantrums:** It will be some time before your baby acquires enough expressive language skills to talk to you about his feelings. You may see your baby stiffen and cry heartily or lie on the floor and kick when tired or hungry, because you took an interesting object away, or for no apparent reason at all. Some babies express these emotions with more intensity than others.
- **Becomes aware of gentle versus rough:** For most of this first year, your baby will have a strong instinct to reach for and grab at interesting objects. While breakable objects should be removed from your baby's play area, this is a great time to teach your baby how to use a single finger to stroke an object or a soft patting motion to use with a pet.

Games and Activities

Going Out

Your baby may be going through a socially anxious phase, but that is no reason to avoid people in general. Minding your p's and q's starts early.

1. Take your baby out into your local community and interact with people as feels natural to you.
2. While interacting, make sure that she hears you using polite words, such as "thank you," "you're welcome," and "please."
3. Don't force your baby to look at strangers and interact. Rather, speak up on behalf of your baby and use the polite words you would like to hear her say someday when being with new people is less intimidating.

Gentle Touches

How should we pet kitty? Soooo gently. It's time to practice safe, respectful touching.

1. Knowing that some objects are more fragile than others will come with experience (expect some broken objects along the way), but you can start now by teaching your baby how to touch in different ways.
2. Hold a fragile object in your hands, such as a leaf or a clean feather.
3. Demonstrate how to lightly touch the object with an index finger while saying the word "gentle."
4. Allow your child the opportunity to imitate the action.

Wipe It Up

Cleaning up a spill is a very useful skill. You might be amazed by your baby's continued interest in an activity that most adults consider a chore.

1. Spray or drip some plain water onto a flat surface, such as a low table or the floor. Describe what it looks like. For example, you might say, "There's a puddle on the floor."
2. Now show him how to wipe with a cloth to soak up the water.
3. When you're finished wiping, repeat the activity so that he can imitate your actions. Some babies like to do this simple action over and over.

Notes

A toy my baby enjoyed choosing this month was . . .

_____

_____

_____

_____

_____

_____

_____

An activity my baby really focused on this month was . . .

_____

_____

_____

_____

_____

_____

_____

YEAR TWO PREVIEW

While there's nothing like your baby's first year of life, one-year-olds are a delight. Here's a preview of some of the things your child will be working on in year two.

Scribbles: If you give a toddler a crayon, he's going to want to scribble with it. The act of putting color or dark lines on a surface will seem downright magical to your child, and holding the crayon and drawing are preliteracy skills. Most children are inspired to try coloring on every surface they can find, including your walls. Tip: Hold off on the markers and begin with just one crayon at a time. Set the limit at "paper only."

Lifts heavy things: Building muscle strength takes a lot of hard work, so you will see your child intentionally choosing things to do that require the absolute maximum amount of effort possible. Toddlers often seek out heavy objects to lift and carry around for the sheer joy of it. Make sure that your child has lots of opportunities to develop this skill.

Builds a tower: Your child will first stack one block on top of another, and then two blocks on top, and as the year progresses, the towers will get higher and higher. And what happens after the tower is so carefully built? Knocking it down, of course, which develops motor skills and illustrates cause and effect.

Climbs: While the more advanced playground equipment will need to wait, your toddler will observe older children monkeying around and want to give it a try. Climbing up a short ladder and going down a slide will be entirely possible for most children in the second year.

Runs: Toddlers are known for having boundless amounts of energy. Once your child becomes fairly coordinated and adept at walking, you are likely to see the pace quicken into a run, first for brief bursts and then for longer periods of racing around in excitement.

Pulls and pushes objects: Your tot will enjoy walking around while pulling a toy by a string (no longer than 12 inches) or a small wagon. Pushing is just as fun. Many toddlers enjoy pushing a doll-size stroller, walker wagon (see "Pushing to Walk" on page 179), or mini grocery cart. Never leave your child unattended with string.

Shows some signs of potty readiness: Some toddlers will become interested in the toilet. Your child might take a diaper on and off, express a need to pee or poop, or practice sitting on a little potty.

Gives a hug to comfort others: Your toddler has spent the first year learning to recognize your emotions. Now she not only recognizes when others are happy or sad but is also able to respond in a socially appropriate way, like hugging someone who is crying.

Imitates adult activities: Your mini me will continue to watch your every move and copy whatever you do. You will see your toddler engaging in some beginning pretend play, such as vacuuming with a stick, nursing a baby doll, or holding a block up to her ear to talk into it like a phone.

Sings songs: While you spent the first year singing lullabies and nursery rhymes to your baby, this year your tot will likely be singing them back to you. So twinkle, twinkle, little tot, you'll be singing songs a lot.

MILESTONES

Motor Skills Checklist

- ☐ Has strong reflexes
- ☐ Turns head side to side while lying on stomach
- ☐ Lifts head for a second while lying on stomach
- ☐ Makes jerky, quivering arm thrusts
- ☐ Keeps hands in tight fists
- ☐ Flops head backward if unsupported
- ☐ Brings hands within range of eyes and mouth
- ☐ Newborn reflexes begin disappearing
- ☐ Movements become more purposeful
- ☐ Lifts up shoulders while lying on stomach
- ☐ Holds head steady while being held upright
- ☐ Keeps head centered and looks straight up while lying down
- ☐ Straightens out legs
- ☐ Kicks energetically
- ☐ Becomes aware of own hands and brings fingers together
- ☐ Holds head steady for longer periods

- ☐ Improved upper body strength
- ☐ Stretching legs and kicking more vigorously
- ☐ Opens and closes hands
- ☐ Grasping, shaking, and swiping with the hands
- ☐ Pushes up on elbows and hands
- ☐ Sits supported
- ☐ Rocks and reaches
- ☐ Bounces on feet
- ☐ Plays with toes
- ☐ Perfects mini pushups
- ☐ Sits tripod-style
- ☐ Rolls over more easily
- ☐ Works hard to reach toys
- ☐ Grasps with two hands
- ☐ Rolls both ways
- ☐ Sits with less support
- ☐ Rakes small objects toward self
- ☐ Coordinates upper-body movements
- ☐ Transfers objects between hands
- ☐ Sits unsupported
- ☐ Assumes the crawling position
- ☐ May show first signs of future pincer grasp

- ☐ Scoots in all directions
- ☐ Shuffles
- ☐ Rocks back and forth
- ☐ Picks up small objects with four fingers and thumb
- ☐ Crawls
- ☐ Stands with support
- ☐ Pulls up to a stand
- ☐ Bangs objects together with two hands
- ☐ Drops objects on purpose
- ☐ Switches positions
- ☐ Pulls to a stand and balances
- ☐ Refines the pincer grip
- ☐ Manipulates objects
- ☐ Learns to release an item voluntarily
- ☐ Sits from a standing position
- ☐ Holds your hand to stand
- ☐ Stands alone for brief periods
- ☐ Cruises around the furniture
- ☐ Empties and fills containers
- ☐ Stoops from a standing position
- ☐ Goes up and down stairs
- ☐ Turns pages of a book
- ☐ Takes first steps

Sensory Development Checklist

- ☐ Focuses 8 to 12 inches away
- ☐ Tracks moving objects at close range (eyes might wander and occasionally cross)
- ☐ Prefers black-and-white or high-contrast patterns
- ☐ Is sensitive to bright light
- ☐ Cries, startles, or quiets with loud noises
- ☐ Has a highly tuned sense of smell
- ☐ Has a well-developed sense of taste
- ☐ Prefers soft sensations
- ☐ Dislikes rough or abrupt handling
- ☐ Focuses on objects moving across field of vision
- ☐ Prefers to look at more complex patterns
- ☐ Prefers colorful patterns
- ☐ Startles in response to unexpected movements and noises
- ☐ Enjoys skin massages
- ☐ Has improved focusing and tracking abilities
- ☐ Develops distance vision
- ☐ Pays attention to small objects
- ☐ Starts using hands and eyes in coordination
- ☐ Turns head toward direction of sound

- ☐ Distinguishes between different colors, tastes, and smells
- ☐ Mouths objects
- ☐ Looks for the source of a sound
- ☐ Studies small items
- ☐ Gazes at objects in the distance
- ☐ Is attracted to bright colors
- ☐ Locates sounds more quickly
- ☐ Is attracted to small items
- ☐ Explores toys with mouth
- ☐ Discerns subtle shades of color
- ☐ Tracks objects with more precision
- ☐ Explores own body
- ☐ Tracks a falling object farther
- ☐ Feels textures with more attention
- ☐ Reacts differently to different voices
- ☐ Enjoys rhythmic movement
- ☐ Tracks rapid movements
- ☐ Is distracted less often
- ☐ Looks for the hidden sources of sounds
- ☐ Examines objects with hand and mouth
- ☐ Practices self-feeding
- ☐ Recognizes people and objects across the room

- ☐ Follows your gaze if you look away
- ☐ Categorizes physical properties of objects
- ☐ Discerns between different tactile sensations
- ☐ Enthusiastically makes noise
- ☐ Enjoys tasting different foods
- ☐ Feeds self with fingers
- ☐ Becomes more aware of heights
- ☐ Quickly identifies faces and objects
- ☐ Concentrates on hearing banging/shaking sounds
- ☐ Feeds self with more skill
- ☐ Conducts purposeful sensory investigations
- ☐ Is less distracted by extraneous noises
- ☐ Views objects from a distance and crawls toward them
- ☐ Has fully developed vision
- ☐ Listens and looks at the same time
- ☐ Tries to alter flimsy objects, such as paper
- ☐ Has increased focus and attention
- ☐ Thrives on human touch
- ☐ Nurses for comfort
- ☐ Returns hugs and kisses
- ☐ Seeks isolated sensory experiences

Language and Mental Development Checklist

- [ ] Cries to communicate needs
- [ ] Turns face away to indicate preferences
- [ ] Calms when held, snuggled, or touched gently
- [ ] May be soothed by low, rhythmic tones
- [ ] Can discriminate among all speech sounds in human language
- [ ] Reaches the peak of crying and starts to cry less
- [ ] Watches movements of parents' lips
- [ ] Begins to coo and gurgle
- [ ] Recognizes familiar objects
- [ ] Anticipates familiar routines
- [ ] Squeals, growls, and coos
- [ ] Laughs out loud
- [ ] Starts razzing (see page 44)
- [ ] Entertains self for brief periods
- [ ] Imitates language sounds
- [ ] Giggles with more predictability during simple games
- [ ] Becomes more aware of your inflection
- [ ] Babbles to self

- [ ] Squeals loudly in delight
- [ ] Laughs and squeals often
- [ ] Repeats single sounds
- [ ] Copies your voice
- [ ] Detects emotions with higher accuracy
- [ ] Becomes aware of cause and effect
- [ ] Looks briefly for a dropped toy
- [ ] Enjoys simple games
- [ ] Differentiates between self and others
- [ ] Giggles more often
- [ ] Repeats single sounds more frequently
- [ ] Responds to own name
- [ ] Becomes aware of the word "no"
- [ ] Babbles chains of consonants
- [ ] Imitates patterns of speech
- [ ] Finds partially hidden objects
- [ ] Understands "no" more clearly
- [ ] Waves bye-bye
- [ ] Interprets gestures
- [ ] Combines different sounds together
- [ ] Looks for you or dropped toys

- [ ] Recognizes and responds to familiar words
- [ ] Verbalizes a few words with meaning
- [ ] Laughs appropriately
- [ ] Searches longer for desired toys
- [ ] Understands a wide variety of words
- [ ] Converses eagerly back and forth
- [ ] Verbalizes a few words
- [ ] Understands brief requests for action
- [ ] Plays finger-pointing vocabulary games
- [ ] Uses gestures, signs, and hand motions with purpose
- [ ] Increases receptive language vocabulary
- [ ] Increases expressive language
- [ ] Practices using known words in context
- [ ] Demonstrates problem-solving skills
- [ ] Responds to one-step commands
- [ ] Responds to simple questions
- [ ] Makes simple choices

Social-Emotional Skills Checklist

- ☐ Prefers the human face to all other patterns
- ☐ Makes eye contact and scans faces for reassurance
- ☐ Favors the sound of high-pitched voices
- ☐ Turns toward familiar sounds and voices
- ☐ Recognizes the scent of own mother
- ☐ Recognizes parents' faces
- ☐ Is soothed and reassured by parents' touch
- ☐ May smile in response to parents' smiles
- ☐ May smile spontaneously to express pleasure
- ☐ Enjoys playing with others
- ☐ Uses facial expressions and body language
- ☐ Maintains eye contact for longer periods
- ☐ Anticipates daily routines
- ☐ Reacts more dramatically to your voice
- ☐ Communicates more clearly
- ☐ Fusses to get your attention
- ☐ Enjoys the company of unfamiliar people
- ☐ Recognizes parent's voice or touch

- ☐ Increases intensity of eye contact
- ☐ Requests playtime
- ☐ Expresses dislikes
- ☐ Anticipates and relies on regular routines
- ☐ Acts more attached to family members
- ☐ Reveals unique personality traits
- ☐ Mimics and shares your emotions
- ☐ Engages in a turn-taking game
- ☐ Studies your reactions to others
- ☐ Craves stimulation
- ☐ Lets you know when a game is over
- ☐ Expresses a variety of emotions
- ☐ Examines images in mirrors
- ☐ Responds to others' emotions
- ☐ Shows hesitance toward nonfamily members
- ☐ Begins testing limits
- ☐ Experiences separation anxiety
- ☐ Tests boundaries impulsively
- ☐ Uses vocalizations and gestures to get attention
- ☐ Objects if you try to take a toy away

- ☐ Greets people with a smile
- ☐ Points at objects
- ☐ Claps hands to express joy
- ☐ Tests limits and observes parental reactions
- ☐ Expresses frustration at restrictions
- ☐ Shows physical affection
- ☐ Closely observes your behavior toward others
- ☐ Imitates the activities of others
- ☐ Watches to make sure you remain close by
- ☐ Initiates the "copycat" game
- ☐ Gives and takes objects
- ☐ Recognizes self in mirror
- ☐ Raises arms to be picked up
- ☐ Exhibits more caution
- ☐ Has consistent, irrational fears
- ☐ Becomes more assertive
- ☐ Demands independence
- ☐ Exhibits cooperative behavior
- ☐ Gets frustrated when hungry or tired
- ☐ May show signs of tantrums
- ☐ Becomes aware of gentle versus rough touching

Doctor's Appointments Checklist

When you go to well-visit appointments, the doctor will be evaluating your baby's general health, including physical development.

ONE MONTH

- ☐ Sucks efficiently
- ☐ Blinks when shown a bright light
- ☐ Focuses on very close moving objects
- ☐ Wiggles limbs
- ☐ Responds to loud sounds

TWO MONTHS

- ☐ Smiles at the sound of your voice
- ☐ Notices own hands
- ☐ Brings hands to mouth
- ☐ Lifts head up when on tummy
- ☐ Crosses eyes occasionally but not all the time
- ☐ Pays attention to new faces

FOUR MONTHS

- ☐ Grasps and holds objects
- ☐ Has lost the Moro reflex
- ☐ Turns head to locate sounds
- ☐ Smiles at people
- ☐ Supports own head
- ☐ Coos or makes sounds
- ☐ Tries to imitate your sounds
- ☐ Brings objects to mouth
- ☐ Pushes down with legs when feet are placed on a firm surface
- ☐ Moves one or both eyes in all directions

SIX MONTHS

- ☐ Reaches for objects
- ☐ Shows affection for caregivers
- ☐ Enjoys being around people
- ☐ Responds to sounds around him
- ☐ Mouths objects
- ☐ Makes vowel sounds ("ah," "eh," "oh")
- ☐ Rolls over
- ☐ Sits with support
- ☐ Smiles spontaneously
- ☐ Laughs or makes squealing sounds

NINE MONTHS

- ☐ Follows objects with both eyes at close (one foot) and far (six feet) ranges
- ☐ Bears weight on legs with support
- ☐ Attracts attention through actions
- ☐ Babbles ("mama," "baba," "dada")
- ☐ Plays simple turn-taking games
- ☐ Responds to own name
- ☐ Recognizes familiar people
- ☐ Looks where you point
- ☐ Transfers toys from one hand to the other

TWELVE MONTHS

- ☐ Crawls
- ☐ Stands when supported
- ☐ Searches for hidden objects
- ☐ Says a single word, such as "mama" or "dada"
- ☐ Uses gestures, such as waving hands or shaking head
- ☐ Points to pictures or objects

LETTERS TO MY BABY

Dear Baby, This Is the Story of Your Birth

A Day in the Life: Three Months

A Day in the Life: Six Months

A Day in the Life: Nine Months

A Day in the Life: Twelve Months

Reasons I Am Grateful for You

_____

_____

_____

_____

_____

_____

_____

_____

Places We Went Together

_____

_____

_____

_____

_____

_____

_____

_____

Games You Wanted to Play Over and Over

First Foods

Things I Learned from You

Your All-Time Favorite Books, Music, and Toys

My Wishes and Dreams for You

RESOURCES

Wisdom about any subject is always a collective, collaborative effort. Here are some useful and inspirational books and websites from people who have both studied and written about early childhood.

Books

- *First Steps in Music for Infants and Toddlers,* John M. Feierabend
- *Games to Play with Babies,* Jackie Silberg
- *Mayo Clinic Guide to Your Baby's First Year*
- *The No-Cry Sleep Solution,* Elizabeth Pantley
- *The Philosophical Baby,* Alison Gopnik
- *Retro Baby,* Anne H. Zachry, PhD
- *Understanding the Human Being,* Silvana Quattrocchi Montanaro, MD
- *What to Expect the First Year,* Heidi Murkoff and Sharon Mazel
- *What's Going On in There?* Lise Eliot, PhD
- *The Womanly Art of Breastfeeding,* Eighth Edition, La Leche League International
- *Caring for Your Baby and Young Child*, Sixth Edition, American Academy of Pediatrics

Websites

- *AidtoLife.org*
- *BabywearingInternational.org*
- *BrainChildMag.com*
- *HealthyChildren.org* (American Academy of Pediatrics)
- *HowWeMontessori.com*
- *TheKavanaughReport.com*
- *MusicTogether.com*
- *KellyMom.com*
- *Mother.ly*
- *WHO.int/childgrowth* (World Health Organization)

INDEX

ACKNOWLEDGMENTS

Sweet Juliette, when you were first born, this book was also being born, and I became an aunt for the first time. I am grateful to Devin and Sarah for letting you be my muse.

This book would not have come to be without the wisdom of many other wonderful people. I'd like to give a special shout-out to my editor, Katie Moore, and the rest of the Callisto Media publishing team for all of your guidance and hard work bringing this book to fruition.

I am so very grateful for my husband, David—love of my life and best daddy ever to our two children, Henry and Jude. I learn more about compassionate parenting from him every day. I'd like to express gratitude for my own parents, who have always encouraged me and supported my work. And I have hugs and more hugs for all of my mama friends whose strong, respectful voices remain in my head as I write and whose words of wisdom no doubt are sprinkled among these pages.

Thank you for sharing your stories and reassuring me along the way.

ABOUT THE AUTHOR

AUBREY HARGIS, MEd, is a parent coach and educational consultant best known for her empathetic approach and appreciation for the magic of childhood. As the founder of the Child Development Institute of the Redwoods, she creates online courses and coaches parents in compassionate discipline techniques and Montessori education. Aubrey lives with her husband and two children under a blanket of San Francisco fog, where the coastal cliffs and nearby redwood trails are always beckoning for another adventure. Visit her online at ChildoftheRedwoods.com.

CPSIA information can be obtained
at www.ICGtesting.com
Printed in the USA
JSHW050710200321
12742JS00002B/16

9 781641 520515